I0111028

The

Year

of the

Poet

June 2014

The Poetry Posse

inner child press, ltd.

The Poetry Posse

Jamie Bond

Gail Weston Shazor

Albert 'Infinite' Carrasco

Siddartha Beth Pierce

Janet P. Caldwell

June 'Bugg' Barefield

Debbie M. Allen

Tony Henninger

Joe DaVerbal Minddancer

Robert Gibbons

Neetu Wali

Shareef Abdur – Rasheed

Kimberly Burnham

William S. Peters, Sr.

General Information

The Year of the Poet
June Edition

The Poetry Posse

1st Edition : 2014

This Publishing is protected under Copyright Law as a "Collection". All rights for all submissions are retained by the Individual Author and or Artist. No part of this Publishing may be Reproduced, Transferred in any manner without the prior **WRITTEN CONSENT** of the "Material Owners" or its Representative Inner Child Press. Any such violation infringes upon the Creative and Intellectual Property of the Owner pursuant to International and Federal Copyright Laws. Any queries pertaining to this "Collection" should be addressed to Publisher of Record.

Publisher Information
1st Edition : Inner Child Press :
intouch@innerchildpress.com
www.innerchildpress.com

This Collection is protected under U.S. and International Copyright Laws

Copyright © 2014 : The Poetry Posse

ISBN-13 : 978-0692232668 (Inner Child Press, Ltd.)
ISBN-10 : 0692232664

$ 12.99

Dedication

This Book is dedicated to

Poetry

&

the Spirit

of our Everlasting Muse.

Poets . . .
sowing seeds in the
Conscious Garden of Life,
that those who have yet to come
may enjoy the Flowers.

F oreword

Friends, Family and Readers

This month we have chosen to have this issue themed "Love and Relationship". Collectively there are 17 different voices included providing their own Poetic takes of the subject. Needless to say i know you will enjoy each individual's perspectives.

Our position is that we choose not to censor the content nor the expressions. This maintains a authenticity in the work and the personal influences of each individual. I found this to be quite interesting, for it exemplifies the diversity of our Humanity and our Poetry. Enjoy . . .

bless up

bill

ps :

don't forget that all issues from January to this date are available as a FREE Download or in Print at Inner Child Press.

Preface

The year of the poet is a collectable collaboration of distinguished artists personally selected to write and publish every month affection ally donned as the poetry posse.

We are honored to have such an elite spectrum of "Pen Mates" along with spotlights of monthly features that you may not have otherwise been introduced to.

The books are all free downloads at inner child press for only 5 dollars for the physical copy. We have made these books affordable to the public, struggling artists, friends, fans and family.

We are proud to present this for your reading pleasure.

Enjoy,

Jamie Bond

Thank God for Poetry
otherwise
we would have a problem !

~ wsp

Table of Contents

The Poetry Posse

Table of Contents . . . *continued*

Poets, Writers . . . know that we are the enchanting magicians that nourishes the seeds of dreams and thoughts . . . it is our words that entice the hearts and minds of others to believe there is something grand about the possibilities that life has to offer and our words tease it forth into action . . . for you are the Poet, the Writer to whom the Gift of Words has been entrusted . . .

~ wsp

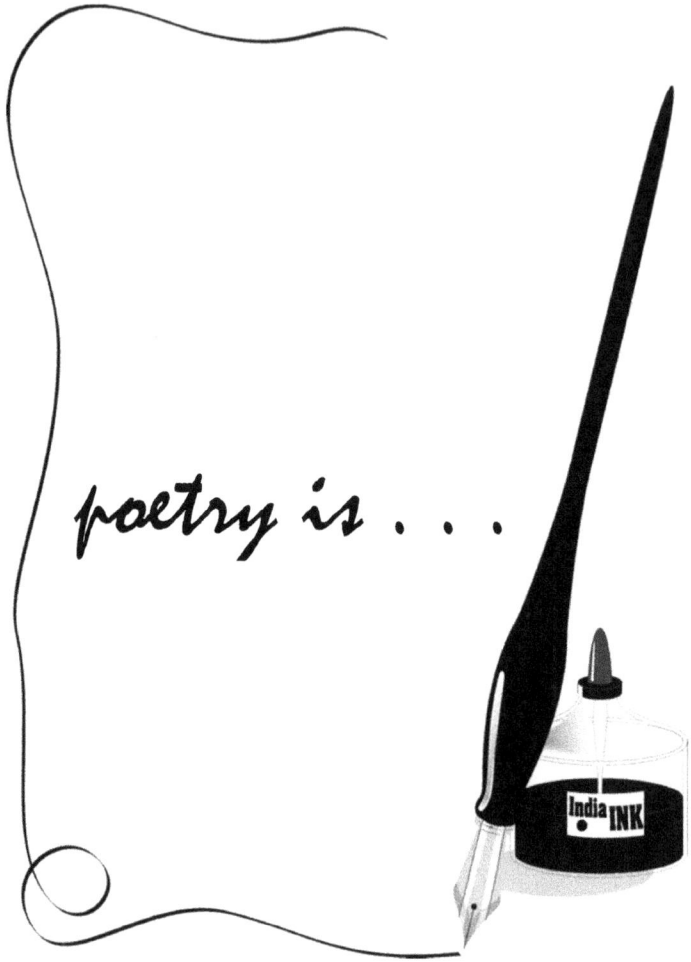

poetry is . . .

The
Year
of the
Poet

June 2014

The Poetry Posse

inner child press, ltd.

Poetry succeeds where instruction fails.

~ wsp

Jamie Bond

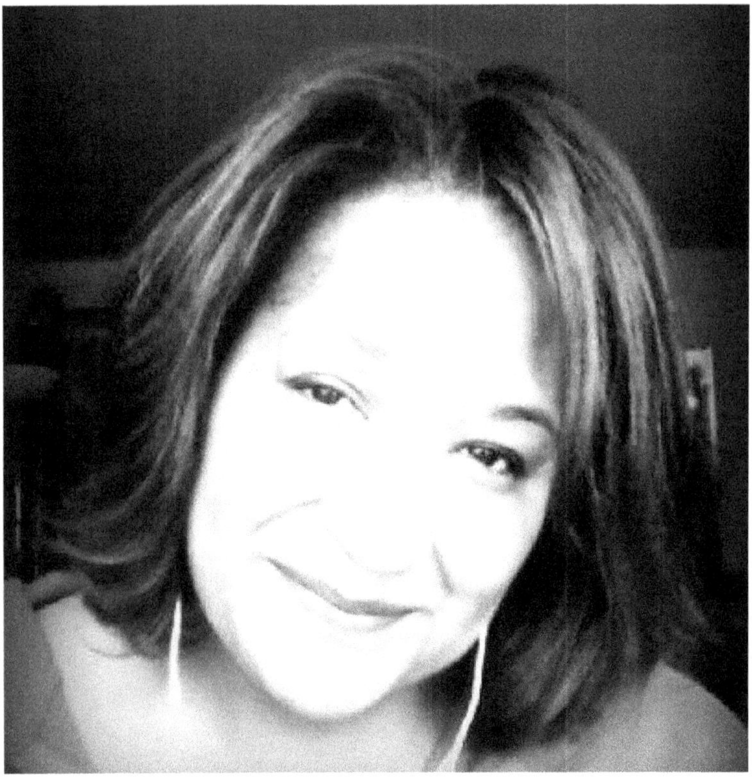

Jamie Bond aka UnMuted Ink is an authoress, radio show hostess, poetess and spoken word maven.

She is; as she says "google-able" if you type in itsbondjamiebond or unmuted ink; you'll find her on various social networks. Born and raised in Brick City aka Newark, NJ. Jamie Bond has been recognized publicly by her peers in various genres for her poetic influences. Her Poetic resume is extensive and her spoken word performances go far beyond 1,000 stage appearances globally. Best known for her networking and marketing skills; her future goals are to become more grounded as a liaison for a variety of fundraisers, activism, volunteering as an advocate as she uses her pen and voice to empower and raise the consciousness of those around her.

Her Motto

Help me to help you to help us... BUT if helping you hurts me, then I can't help you!

http://www.facebook.com/IBJB.BrickCity

Literary Love, Literally Love

Let love be our downfall
With you I'm willing to risk rise
Be on some ride or die type shit
I want to roll the dice, shoot the shit
And throw darts with you boo
I want to be your favorite poem
And create haikus with you

Recite me like my emotions were
Your personal mic let me be your stage
Take your time… Be a slow Tanka
And let me be your long lived sonnet

I want to monologue
Whisper spoken words
That slide into your earlobes
Then disappear into the ether …
Like the aroma of something being sautéed

I want to structure soliloquies
With disappearing ink on invisible paper
While you dedicate me a simile
Cuz you ODE me one anyway from yesterday

The thought of being a
Conjunction to your adjectives
All natural no preservatives
While I'm the noun to your pronouns
While we make verbs together
Let me be the descriptive color you adore
Let me scribe forevermore
As my everlasting moments with you

I want to be the free verse
Inside of your structured quatrain
Create limerick couplets
And breathe 16 bars of Cinquain
The way you adore me
Easily doubling our heartbeats
In 5 syllabic moments
Like a collaborative masterpiece
For an audience of two
Let me intimately interview you

You are the shape of my favorite number
Let me spell it with my tongue on you
I want to add something spectacular
To your vernacular
You can be the something special
To my sweet nothings on a pedestal
Let me express myself without words
Like your private dancer with adverbs

And if iron sharpens iron then it's on
Let's work out and take showers together
Let's re-create legends and win slams together
Under the perspiration of a passionate blanket

Fulfilled day dreams
of naming colossal stars after you
Unbreakable bonds ... like love's scar is a tattoo
I want to read you like my favorite book
Speak to me in signals and touch me to the core
With your expressions
make us the exception of literary love,

I need your actions to be implicit lyrics
… no really; literally love

Here are my passwords and keys
because actually I trust you with me
So no need to ask me
here's the combination lock code to me and you
Respect so true …just maybe…
maybe… I could salute you

Titleholder

Let me…
Nurse your battle wounds on a daily basis
…like the sacred aloe that rebuilds and maintains your
masculinity
Be the supplement that your body needs to thrive

I want to nourish your contemplations
And be the balanced meal you consume in appropriate
proportions
Enrich your soul with only the finest increments of protein
based calories
So that you can get fat on love

While the art of love making is your sole appetite
suppressant
…And a saved day by my hero is anxiously defined as
You happily coming home to me

I want to…
Remind you to reminisce on the skill of loving yourself
More than you could ever love me
And keep on repeat like a CD that never skips
…While reminding you to be my best friend
As you out do yourself every day without hesitation of
Ever feeling torn between separating your wants from your
needs

I want to be…
The unwritten pages in your novel of dreams
And weave wishes come true into a mesh of introspection
with you….
Jam packed with archaic but captivating facts and secrets
about you

Write me rescued by your arms
Let me read you a love story starring US….
And let's liquidate our assets to each other's highest bids
Like an estate auction

Please DO…
Flip thru me like your favorite used bible
Where the tattered pages are so dog eared
That they jump into your palms
Singing psalms into your eyes while catching your smile
I want to be the bold tipped rainbow accent highlighter
….To the words only you can underline inside of my soul

A Love so simple and pure
That infatuation and puppy love become an abiding
addiction…

And if only…
If only we could bottle our kisses
As if high doses of adoration and reverence
Were the cures for cancer… And become millionaires
In sharing what WE have together with the world
To make it a better place….

I need you
To be my nocturnal training coach …
If only you'll allow me be your doctoral champion
I want to be your invention while you allow me to patent
you
As if what we have here;
Were the winning lottery tickets …
…with a lifetime pension…

YES WE CAN Mr. Man...

Put these covers over your head
Like a voting booth
And push all of my secret buttons
And then pull the lever...

...Wear a suit tonight
And be a persuasive politician
Connect with me...
Understand why I need to believe

...Create careers,
Give healthy raises and benefits packages
Provide homeland security jobs in the bedroom...
And a small business incentive...

...Court me with fawning words,
Use chivalry as your upper hand
Against my defense mechanisms....

...Serenade me with sweet nothings
Like a politically correct Democrat
Desperately trying to obtain leverage
To sway a skeptical Republican's vote....

...Let's go on a statewide campaign
Exclusively implementing family values...

...Be my President and I'll be your First Lady
As you take an oath and solemnly swear
Into my ovarian office...

As my actions toward you become
A memorized speech embedded on your lips
And every night I re-erect you
With an unarguably beautiful inauguration speech
Inside of my lips......

sigh Sweetheart....
You got my vote for a maximum term ♥

Gail

Weston

Shazor

This is a creative promise ~ my pen will speak to and for the world. Enamored with letters and respectful of their power, I have been writing for most of my life. A mother, daughter, sister and grandmother I give what I have been given, greatfilledly.

Author of . . .

"An Overstanding of an Imperfect Love"

available at Inner Child Press.

www.facebook.com/gailwestonshazor

www.innerchildpress.com/gail-weston-shazor

navypoet1@gmail.com

Thunder and Lightening

Sterling flashes against green
Where just a sliver of light
Finds its way into loam
The depression created
By thunder bounces
Against the sky erratically
And I reach for your hand
Winding my breath around
The forefinger and thumb
Because I want my heart held

We talk of sex
With the honesty of expectations
That occur naturally and with a
Spontaneity in a lifetime
Of familiarity
Time has no hold on this
Our kinetic friendship
Because I knew you
Long before I was meant
For you to find in places unlooked

It is here in the darkest moments
With your back against
The sturdy spine of trees
I can fit inside the palms
That rest against the bent hip
Of my softness, gentleness
The coaxing of calmness
Against the temperance of a quickening
And I am no longer alone
Within this lightening storm

I keep hidden those words
Said in haste but always
Measured against the moment
Of someone else's parting
Of our enclosed solitude
The pain of which has faded
In learning what is important about
My heart locked into the space
Between thumb and forefinger
And yours ever in my soul

Longhand

I write longhand most days

With a thought to how long

My ink will last

It can be somewhat intelligible

And somewhat reliable

The thoughts I leave

The memories

I struggle to hold onto

Crayoning and penciling in

The fraying edges with preciousness

Did you actually taste so sweet

For my lips ache to take you

Even now my knees part for you

I remember that your voice

Could make the angels weep

And the taste of key limes make me laugh.

Float On

There is a little boat floating
In the center of the gutter
Held upstream by the loud voices
That clatter in disagreement
Over the size and whiches of the things
That have gotten through the dam
And the discordance ebbs and flows
With each coronation and each rewrite
The truth is held hostage on the tide
Or maybe is just turbulence
The little boat heeds not the changes
As little boats tend to not pay
Much attention to anything other than wind
And other vessels of any sort

There is a little boat floating
Upstream from the flotsam and jetsam
It defies the man made waves
That attempt to push it into the compliance
Of one book or another
One edict or another that the noise
Grows more and more excited about
And the boat can only be moved
By the breath of the creator
That blows down through the gutter
Like bumper guards for bumper cars
Because the clatter has put up safeguards
Against the truth that life is simple
And all the rules and regulations
Are not of the breath of life
But obligations made to each other

There are little boats floating
Upstream in a gutter
And they may seem deceptively small
Like little mustard seeds adrift
Small refuges in a vast seas of waters
One of kind to each other
When the gutter is awash
The boats simply drift, trusting
That the breath will keep the course
While the din raises alarm
And more rules are passed awaiting them
To become big boats with important sails
That can make more laws to govern boats
Separate themselves into classes
And colors and even manufacturers
Waiting for them to amiss their true purpose
Of being guided for dream carrying
There are little boats floating, waiting
In the gutters, for you to be their dams

If you sacrifice your art because of some woman, or some man, or for some color, or for some wealth, you can't be trusted.

- Miles Davis

Albert

Infinite

Carrasco

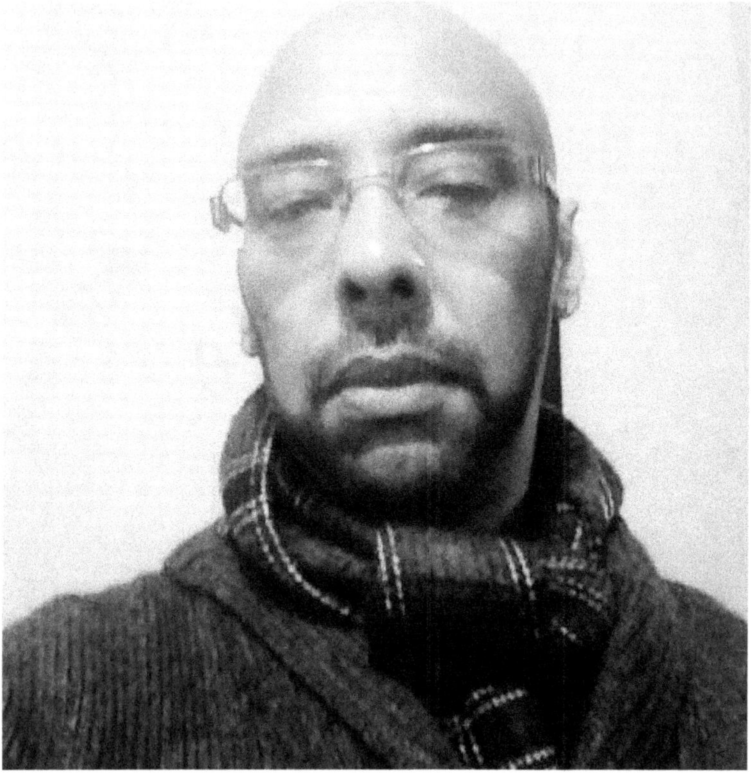

Albert Carrasco writes hieroglyphics encrypted in poetic form. His linguistics are not the norm. When it comes to wisdom, sleet ,rain snow and hail its a lyrical storm. He's pure like Fiji, he got the power to hear the dead with no auji. For living a life so tabu, He learnt a die-a-lect , his mouth moves... But at times it's the voice of the crossovers coming through. When he's on stage he has a body temp of 98 degrees... When He recites you feel this chilling breeze, hair stands on skin when he's in the avatar state of his kin. He's non traditional, an unorthodox outspoken urban individual that lived through the subliminal, now he's back to give guidance to his people.

Infinite the poet 2014

Infinite poetry @lulu.com

Alcarrasco2 on YouTube

Infinite the poet on reverbnation

The Poems this month are from my Book
Infinite Poetry
available at
http://www.lulu.com/us/en/shop/al-infinite-carrasco/infinite-poetry/paperback/product-21040240.html

I should've kissed her

I should of kissed her. I should of told her how I felt, for holding back my two cents I'm now broke.. My heart that is. For being a shy brother I lost her, why o why didn't have the power of Cupid to just passionately shoot her. Now she's like the wind.. Breezed right by. I think of how it would've of been holding, touching, caressing.. If I would of spoken. Please mother nature blow her back to me my heart is suffering it's an emergency, I, I, I..need her here with me. She's so beautiful in all aspects, it's hard to breathe when I think of her, she's breathtaking. She got me like a jonesing asthmatic.

If I get a second chance I'll make a great first impression, I know she'll work for me, I'll pay her with undivided attention, steamy love sessions, her nick name will be nevaeh cause I'm going to make her feel like she's in heaven... After I kiss her

Georgie Porgie

I have a problem,
i try to control it.
whenever a queen is around it consumes me, its called love
and affection.
When I'm near the most beautiful thing the heavens
invented, I worship it.
She can be just a friend, I still want to hold her little hands,
Theirs compliment mines.
I still want to lay with them,
To be embraced by wisdom.
We don't need to make love, just talk to me baby,
A sweet voice sexes my pituitary.
I just enjoy a lady.
Now if I have an attraction for you, and you for me, it'll be
a trip..
Cause I know you'll fall.
Ill hold you tightly and smother your mouth with my full
lips,
My manly hands will explore curvature,
As my green eyes dampens inner thighs,
I'm a touchy feely type of brother,
I touch deeply, so they can feel me,
Skeet before me, Im no stingy lover.
They call me Georgie porgy,
Not cause I make them cry, then run away,
They cry cause they want me around every second of the
day.

I need you

I need to hold you squeeze you caress you, I need you.
I'm overwhelmed with your beauty, your sincerity, your warmth.
You comfort me.
So relaxed I feel in your company.
As I lay my head on your thighs and stare up at your eyes, I feel a connection.
I feel a chill in my bones, your my love jones.
Your touch I wait in anticipation.
I know you still feel the same.
With me you can have it all,
Love
Affection
Undivided attention
The best love making sessions.
I gave you my last name to start a generation,
A cluster formation,
I'm the sun your the moon, we created some stars.
Your the queen in my fantasies, don't need to pinch myself to see that I'm dreaming,
I just pucker up and let you kiss me.
What a feeling!
Such a perfect sculpture,
flawless
That 3 karat diamond surrounded by baguettes,
Ensures me no other brother will ever get to feel that feeling you give me
I love you .

Author Infinite the poet
Albert carrasco
lulu.com infinite poetry

Siddartha

Beth

Pierce

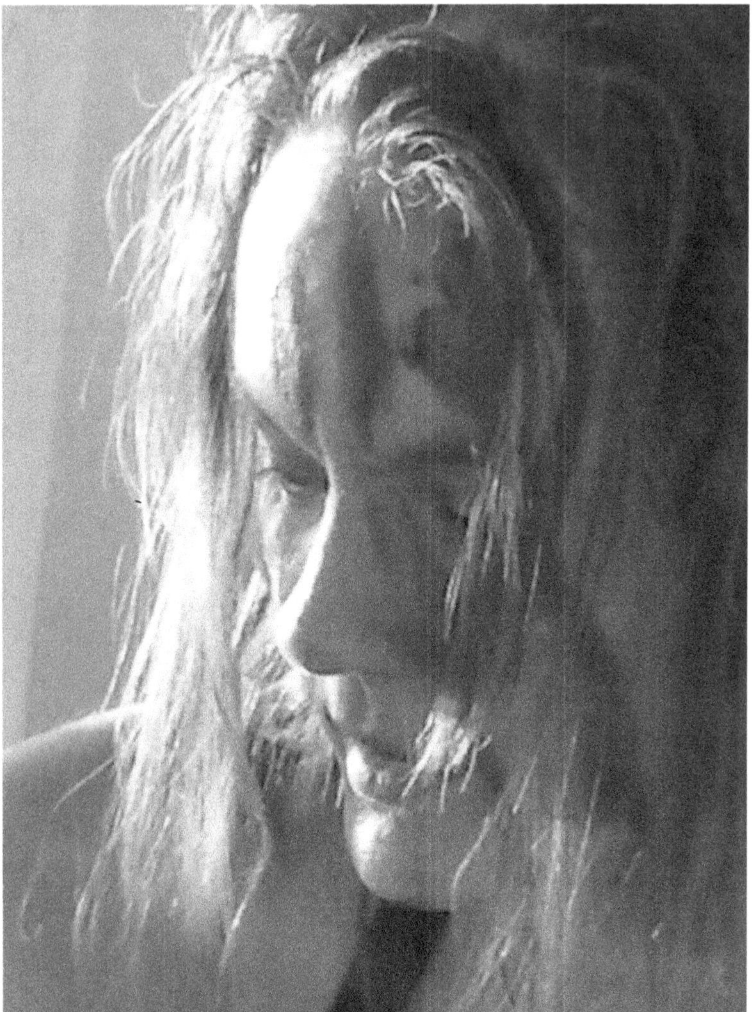

Siddartha Beth Pierce is a Mother, Poet, Artist and African and Contemporary Art Historian. Her art, poetry and teaching were featured on PBS in April 2001 while she was the Artist-in-Residence and Associate Professor at Virginia State University in Petersburg, Virginia. She received her BA in Studio Art from George Mason University in Fairfax, Virginia and her M.A.E. from Virginia Commonwealth University in Richmond, Virginia. She continued into PhD. Studies in African and Contemporary Art studies at Virginia Commonwealth University where she is now All but Dissertation. Her works of poetry and art have been featured in numerous newspaper articles, journals, magazines and chapbooks.

http://www.innerchildpress.com/siddartha-beth-pierce.php

http://www.youtube.com/watch?v=OQ87NrLt_to

http://www.writerscafe.org/Siddartha

Apart From You

With you
I am often
at a loss for words
to express
the depth of
my devotion.

Apart from you
I long to be
near you again
as soon as
possible.

With you
I have the strength
to conquer any
obstacle that
may come my way.

Apart from you
I still feel your
strong embrace
about me
carrying me
through my days.

With you
I am Love
itself
personified
through your sweet
smile.

Apart from you
I wait
for the next time
that we will
be together
again
and I will be
whole
once more.

Bliss

On this day,
sealed with a kiss
the wedded bliss
begins.

Anew,
Refreshed,
entrenched
as One
their Union
shall be Blessed
as always and ever shall be.

On this day,
sealed with a kiss
the wedded bliss
begins, Anew.

Love,
Divines the Air
the words are shared
to bind them together always,
I Do.

Keeper of the Garden
for Garth Foster

You are a shining star,
the moon, the sun
warming the greenery,
as well as my heart.

My soul sings
when you are in the room.

You, are the keeper
of this garden of Love
that is blossoming forth
between us.

A nod, a smile
from you, beguiles
and a garden springs
eternally forth
with recollections,
hopes and dreams
that you, the keeper
of the garden shall
never leave my side.

But rest still
he here with me,
beneath the galaxies
tending to this burgeoning
Love, my dearest,
Keeper of the garden.

Janet

Perkins

Caldwell

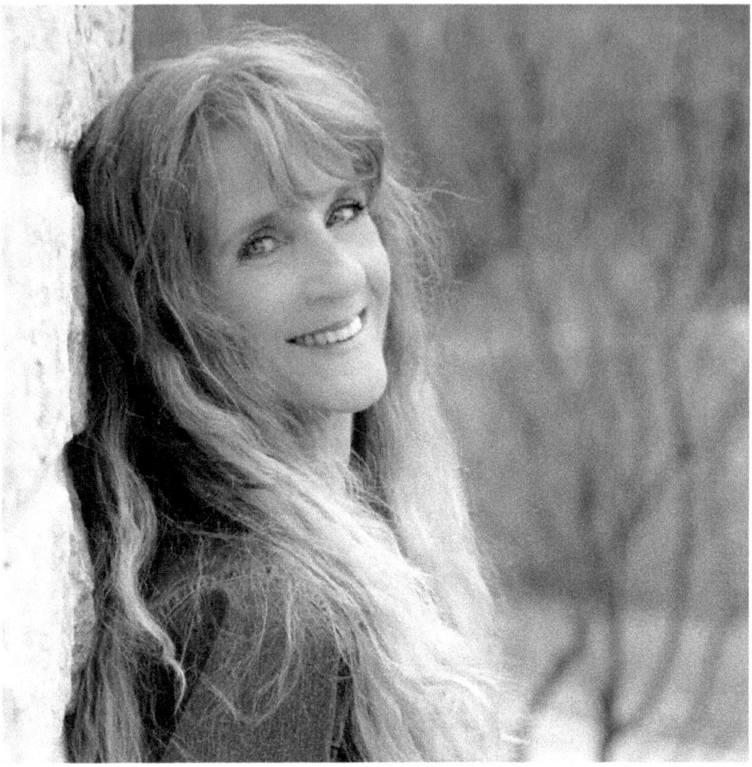

Janet wrote her first poems and short stories in an old diary where she noted her daily thoughts. She wrote whether suffering, joyful or hoping for peace in the world. She started this process at the tender age of Eight. This was long before journaling was in vogue.

Along with her thoughts, poetry and stories, she drew what she refers to as Hippie flowers. Janet still to this day embraces the Sixties and Seventies flower power symbol, of peace and love, which are a very important part of her consciousness.

Janet wrote her first book, in those unassuming diaries, never to be seen by the light of day due to an unfortunate house fire. This did not deter her drive. She then opted for a new batch of composition journals and filled everyone. In the early nineteen-eighties, Janet held a byline in a small newspaper in Denton, Texas while working full time, being a Mother and attending Night School.

Since the early days Janet has been published in newspapers, magazines and books globally. She also has enjoyed being the feature on numerous occasions, both in Magazines, Radio and on a plethora of Sites. She has gone on to publish three books. *5 degrees to separation* 2003, *Passages* 2012 and her latest book *Dancing Toward the Light . . . the journey continues* 2013. All of her Books are available through Inner Child Press along with Fine Book Stores Globally. Janet P. Caldwell is also the Chief Operating Officer of Inner Child ltd.

http://www.janetcaldwell.com/

http://www.innerchildpress.com/janet-p-caldwell.php

https://www.facebook.com/JanetPCaldwell

June Weddings & Such

The month and the year was June, 2014
when the culmination of
frolicking lover's days
were winding down.

D
O
W
N

to a ritualistic
life-time trip
walking man's commitment aisle.

She approached her man
with tears in her eyes
a silent begging seen
please let us just run away
and stay just the way
that we are.

There is no need
for all of the fanfare.
Thousands of dollars spent
and for what, to satisfy the masses ?

As a matter of fact
we were wed
long before and our ceremony
was very private.

I love and want you
that should be enough.
No papers needed
you did give a ring
as a token of your love
for me . . .

and most importantly
you gave of yourself
as I did you, yes my love
no man's certificate is needed.
You see, we are one in spirit, indefinitely.

(c) May 7th, 2014 Janet P. Caldwell

We Came

You may come to love me hard again
to revel in coitus, simply rapturous
mmmmm, with our bodies interfaced.

Resonant and guttural voices
vibrating from times passed
yes, you may come.

Our spirits are now as One
on the eve of this horizon
since you and I have risen above the madness.

We have come to delight in life's simple pleasures
finding in each other, life's treasures
we have arrived, we sang, we danced . . .

we came . . . again.

(c) May 7th, 2014 Janet P. Caldwell

Notebooks

My notebooks are filled
with half poems, ideas
some brilliant and then
there are the others . . .

I see my Mother in one
she, with her olive skin
dark auburn hair
and a heart so big
that it could not be contained.

I see my God, the notes
and prayers unanswered.
They say . . .
I am supposed to be glad for this.

I see my daughter
her adult ways
and it blows my mind
that she is truly my child.

I see my son and his soft heart
the wife and children that he loves so
and I wonder, how did I get so lucky ?

Wait ! I don't believe in luck.
I am blessed somehow
despite my craziness

that these two turned out
finer than *any* wine, yes
some - ONE is looking out for us.

I see lovers, lost and gained
joy and pain, the tears and rainy days
reckless lives abandoned once
only to be *re-saved.*

I see me and wonder who *I AM*
then a stirring moves deep inside
and I know, I am another page
in this *Universal's notebook stage.*

(c) May 7th, 2014 Janet P. Caldwell

June
'Bugg'
Barefield

June 'Bugg' Barefield

June Barefield ~ Poet-Activist-Teacher-Author

Born and raised in the Midwest, currently residing in East St Louis, IL. Junes interests include long walks, sunrises, cheesecake, and words. He considers the NRA, and it's supporters 2B a 21st century Nazi-ism! The author of two collections of poetry which include B4 the Dawn, and The Journeyman

I B. Self educated, and proud to be humbled. An avid reader, and teacher, counselor in his community at what we as a society have termed "at risk children". June refers to them as Gang members, and dope dealers. A brilliant speaker, and motivator; fluent in at least three religions! June's favorite quote: "FUCK THE SYSTEM!"

for booking call : 720 404 8563

http://authorsdb.com/authors-directory/2292-june-barefield

you can get more of June here . . ,

https://www.facebook.com/JuneBugg900

https://www.facebook.com/june.barefield.7

http://www.innerchildpress.com/june-barefield.php

LOVE

What is it
Beauty or bitterness
Flattery or forgiveness?

LOVE.

I wonder...
Does it grieve or feel guilt
LOVE.

Will it blossom or wilt?
LOVE IZ LOYALTY
love won't lie
Love is life, but sometimes...
LOVE DIES.

LOVE.

Is it the future
or has love passed?
It's just gotta be the look on all of these faces out here
when my pockets are full of cash!
LOVE CAN KISS MY ASS.

LOVE.

Jack; He just loves that ole' car &
Jill; That bitch would murder nations 2B a movie star!
Love don't love nobody, hardly

LOVE.

Another bourbon bartender, please...
Sitting here again wondering if love can save me
I mean...
What is it?
This Love thing
Temptation, trouBle, trust, talent
Pride, punishment, patience, peace
PLEASE!!!

I Love You.
Do you Love me?

I think I love you

I hope that's not a thought that causes you to run away
I remember when I knew you
We were children then
Do you remember when I thought I was grown?
On my own me thinks...
WAAAAAAY to early in this
Sorta, kinda got caught up in the twist
But, I think I loved you back then too!
And, I believe God Himself had a plan 4 me
to go thru all the shit I been through;then return me
2 you in one piece, and find PEACE in your arms and
embrace
To teach me GRACE,
and faith
and HOPE
& love
YUP.
I think I do...
LOVE YOU.

Gotta know love

To fall in love you gotta know love, but
How can one fall N love; if ONE'S never been shown
Grown
& still searching.
Hurting
Working.
seeking & searching

To fall in love you gotta know hate's worthless

I have fallen...
In love
But
Love never did love me back
Tried to do the right things, and maintain my strong back
Had to retract that
In fact I fell out of love, because the word don't fit the
glove
Shoved TRUTH aside
created my own truth
Sutured up my reality

Made love a technicality

and Now...

Somebody.

I mean somebody besides my own...

TELL ME!

What the fuck is LOVE?

& if I'm a slave to love, can I still maintain my own???

MY MOTHER TOLD ME THAT ONCE LOVE IZ

STITCHED

it's sewn.

She said...

U have got to "KNOW" love.

~4 MOMMA rip 12 Mar2014 ⚘

Debbie
M.
Allen

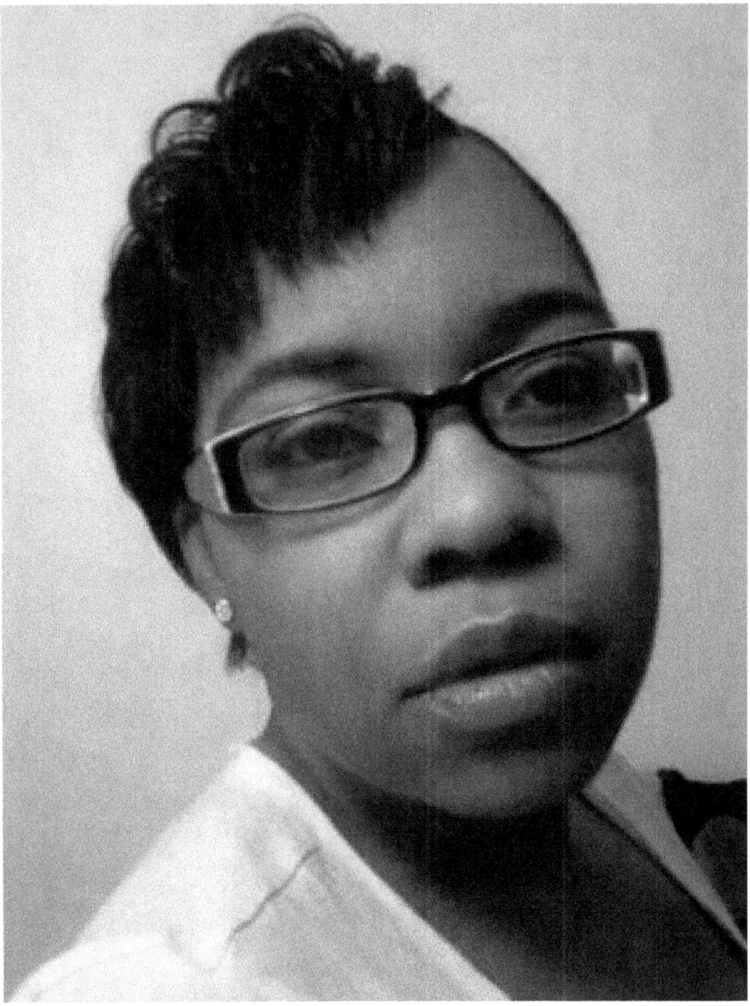

Debbie M. Allen is a Pennsylvania native that has remained true to her passion for the love of poetry. She has always had a passion for poetry. In 2010 she took that passion and made it her cause, always maintaining the truth of her experiences and the beliefs she holds dear.

Debbie is the Author of "A Poet Never Dies," her first book of poetry which was published in 2012. Since then she has published her second book of poems, "The Spiral of a Pisces: In Manic Flow," which encompasses her ever spiraling transition of expression. She can be found participating in various avenues of spoken word and poetry under the pseudonym D. Flo'essence including The Truth Commission Movement, Penology Ink Productions, Jersey Radical Productions and What's The News.

He Balanced Me

There were times when I wondered where my heart went...
Cold on summer nights...when lonely didn't sit right
With me...
Hungry after a full Sunday meal
Contemplating what the deal was with being empty still...
But God knows how to fill
Love is not a platter on dietary distill...
It grows with faith
And there is no haste in that...
Even when light rotates the rainbow back to black...
After all I should be used to that
Hard is the color that has to cover all the slack
Retro vibes beating my heart to retract in...
Into disco lights that high beamed me
Into blinding reflections of reality....
But I reached HIM...
Hand over hand...walked gently
Into the Promised Land...
Life on Earth written in foot printed sand
So when I say I love you now...
Kingdoms bow down
Because they know love is worthy...
No hurt to cause curve in me...
Just worthy...
Founded in destruction
And molded to serve thee...
And so he blessed me
Blessed me in the holding of light
Me...a man...and unity in the fight
To be more than what is seen
And more of what is believed....

The Art of a Smile

Early morning thoughts clear slowly…
Until I see the striking design
Time memorized of your smile,
Brainwaves bouncing along the curve of your lips…

It's been awhile…

Since waking to the sunshine of a newfound day
Expounding the rifting of light
To hinder the flight upon stresses' lost wings
That I believed I would fly the era of age with …
But the rainbow of your aura is one of conquest
High above the dusk of my distress

So waking is blessed with the art of love…

Mixing color into the palate of life
Blush strokes tinting right
Over the black and white of wrongs,
Regrets no longer belong in my masterpiece
I've wisped dawn upon the upset of my valley…
Became a ballet of airbrushed whimsy
Flown across the canvas of living
Painting things bright again…

Every time I remember your smile…

In Pose of None

I been walkin too many steps in the wrong direction
Misinterpreting roses as the objective
To unfolding my hesitations
One petal at a time...
He love me, he love me not kind of
Childish rhyme...
But we all grow up in cold weather...
With strait jackets keeping chilly thoughts from catching
Our sanity on frosty days...
But pleather only keeps us warm
On nights when ours dreams survive past
The real of frigid ways...
So I took him in my arms like the soft of fresh leather
Inhaled him through the thick veil that
Keep me a secret from the teal hue
Of smooth blue skies...
I awoke from lullabies
With R&B on my shoulders...
Heavy in the armor of drums...
That rolled the curses off me
Into I told ya I would be better...
The love inside of me was a go getter
So I got him...
Got him on my knees
Folded in prayers of poetry
One line at a time...
Hooked him in the crook of my verse-book
With renewed quotes that broke...
Every boundary I ever wrote into my life...
A willing sacrifice...
Now I grip him like a vice and with every gasping
Of my lungs wield him some

Of my fight…
It's only right that I give back
What he gave me in my desertion of self
It may not be typical wealth but
It runs plenty…
I and he may course in the crowded dementias of many
Yet we only soldier for one…
Simple equation…
1x1=1 plus none
That is the rogue theory
For a strong ceiling that holds storms
From the plunge….
No rainy days will wash us asunder…
Because if ever we were to go under it will
Be under the sun of our daily run with each other…
So it's settled as I settle myself
Within his scene…
If there is anything I know…
Fuck a motive
And the credits of a played out lover's theme
It just seems was it is
And is what it streams
Like water….
Ever flowing…ever clashing
Ever motivating in the lasting of all things
Especially love….

Tony Henninger

Tony Henninger

Tony has been writing for about 20 years. He has published one book titled " A Journey of Love." He has also contributed to several Anthologies. His book is available at Innnerchild Press and Amazon.com.

You can find him at Facebook.com/Tony Henninger

Linkdin.com/Tony Henninger or

tonyhenninger@yahoo.com

You And Me

Beautiful Lady of Love's wonder,
how my heart pulsates in your
gentle hands, so delicate.

Delightfully smooth caresses
leaving me utterly helpless,
wishing to die in your arms.

Oh, my love, take all of me,
again, and again, and again.
Time and space have no meaning
for those lost in eachother.

Let love be all we see and hear.
Our senses to the ultimate
ecstasy reach and ever be.

You and me
in our own heaven
for all eternity.

I Can Only Dream You

Wandering through the shadows
as the sun slowly sets in the west.
Another day of searching for you,
another night of a dreams unrest.
Each day I miss you more.
Each night I crave your caress.
Why did you leave me behind?
Why did you leave me such a mess?
I know you had no choice.
I know you tried really hard.
I know you are beyond the horizon,
while I'm here with my broken heart.
Maybe you can't reach for me?
Maybe your tears are the rain?
Maybe you are still with me,
trying to ease my pain?
I wish I could see you.
I wish I could feel you.
I wish I could hear you.
I wish I could take your hand.
But, I can only dream you,
I must follow where it leads.
Travel each day to its end
to where dreams and lovers meet.
Where broken hearts can mend.
Where loneliness is no more.
Where souls can be together
forevermore.

To this dream I cling tightly….

Love Me Forevermore

You are my every woman.
You are my every desire.
You are the only one
who sets my soul on fire.

Your soft, silky, skin.
Your love I breathe in.
Tell me what to do
as I move all over you.
It is your sweetness I crave.

Come, make me your slave.
Tell me your every need
as our ecstasies meet.
No inhibitions.
No defenses.
Let me heighten
all of your senses.

I want to make you sweat.
I want to make you regret
when I stop ere release
to make you say "please".

Like the sky bursting with rain
You cherish the pleasure and pain.
And when you can't take anymore,
I know you will love me,

forevermore.

....

Joe
Da Verbal
MindDancer

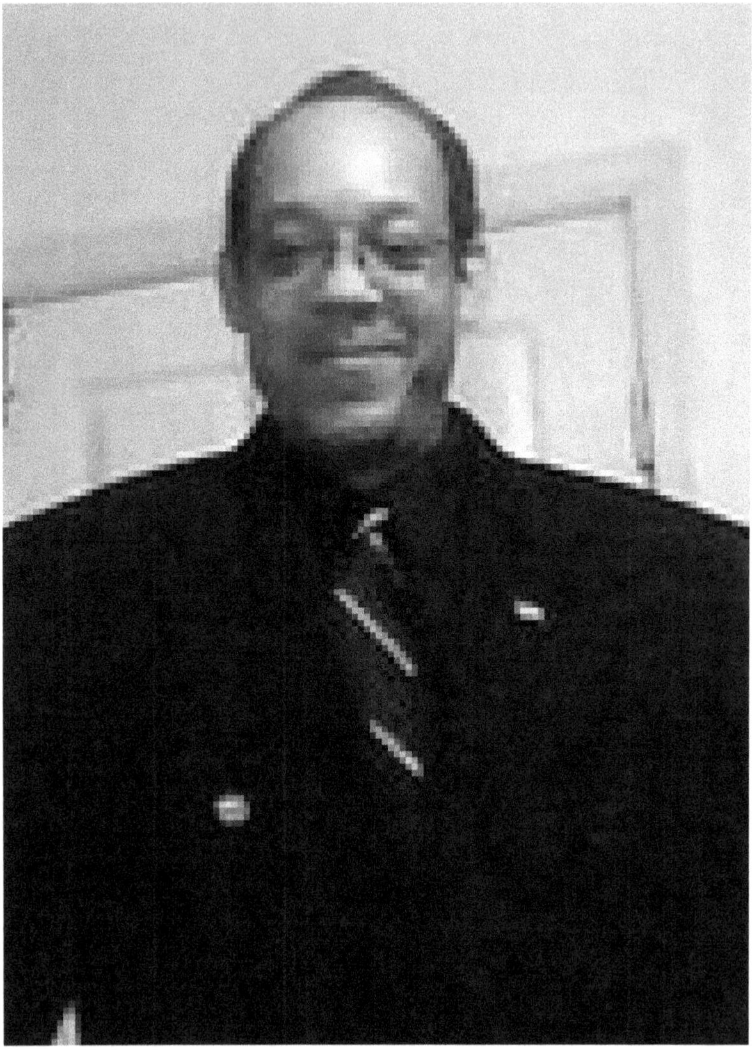

Joseph L Paire' aka Joe DaVerbal Minddancer . . . is a quiet man, born in a time where civil liberties were a walk on thin ice. He's been a victim of his own shyness often sidelined in his own quest for love. He became the observer, charting life's path. Taking note of the why, people do what they do. His writings oft times strike a cord with the dormant strings of the reader. His pen the rosined bow drawn across the mind. He comes full-frontal or in the subtlest way, always expressing in a way that stimulate the senses.

https://www.facebook.com/joe.minddancer

All About Love

There were flowers on the staircase and trailing vines
Lace doilies on patterned armrests; in a dimly lit parlor
I sat in the yellow glow waiting for that first sight.
A homey stench; reeked of goodness
Grandma's cooking was in the stove.
I tried to entertain a conversation; just small talk
A little insight to me;
In hopes of giving comfort and trust.
I was about to take away their loving daughter
I was about to take away what I'd grown to love.

An embarrassing yell of her name I'm sure
Brought her swiftly to the edge of stairs
The unsure sound of her footing,
echoed as she descended from her lair.
I arose in greeting, placing a trimmed rose in her hand.
We were left to speak in our own tongue
Though gentlemanly and lady like
There was that oomph of admiration.
Stolen moments added to the fire building in us.

Grandma would peep in;
to save a virginity long lost to passions kiss
We broke bread along with family
Although our plan was a night out
Love spilled over into that room, want took a back seat
Desire wrapped up like my take home plate.
If love means wait, then I'll wait
If love means being flexible, then I'll stretch
And share what time I have, for love is being there
No matter change of plans.

It's The Little Things

Calling when there is absolutely nothing to say
Fixing a broken lock on a treasured jewelry box
Sitting through hours of recorded soaps
Going to the mall as she tries on everything
Biting your lip as she complains about the silliest things
Saying I LOVE YOU past arguments sting
Getting up to make a sandwich in the middle of the night
Complimenting; before those awaiting eyes
Being supportive when tears fall.
Understanding it's not jealousy,
if she wants you all to herself.

Strong bonds lead to questionable behavior
Do yourself a favor, don't ask why.
Cancelations are matters of fact;
It is how you react that counts as those little things.
Hold tight the hand you love.
Squeeze firmly when you give that hug.
Little girls stay inside the frame of womanhood
Learn how to hold the reins.
Freedom is never feeling the walls of restriction
Nor is restriction a contradiction
Sometimes you have to step in
For those little things, you'll be thanked as a friend.
Relationships are complicated entities.
They have a life of their own; take care of the little things
Love becomes full blown.

Beyond Definition

The most complicated word in any language
        LOVE
I've tried to explain it metaphorically, philosophically
Even with reason, it can't be done.
So many greeting cards with quotable quibble
There are online pages with ways to say it.
Special days to display it; it's outrageous.
Thousands of songs, plays put on
By a not so happy couple trying to save face
Love is just a mask put in place to erase heartache
It's fake.

Used as a noun, a pronoun adverb adjective
Selective is what it is, introspective is what it is
Rejected in it's truest form;
by those who know pain as the norm.
Even a newborn can be hated by it's Mother.
Love is surely not automatic, pragmatic at best.
Love is deceptive; cryptic; Most definitely not forever.
Love is fair-weather or nothing at all.
Yet we cry over it; die over it..
Plot and tell lies over it, as if it were tangible.
It is but a dream, an emotion made alive.

Robert
Gibbons

Robert Gibbons

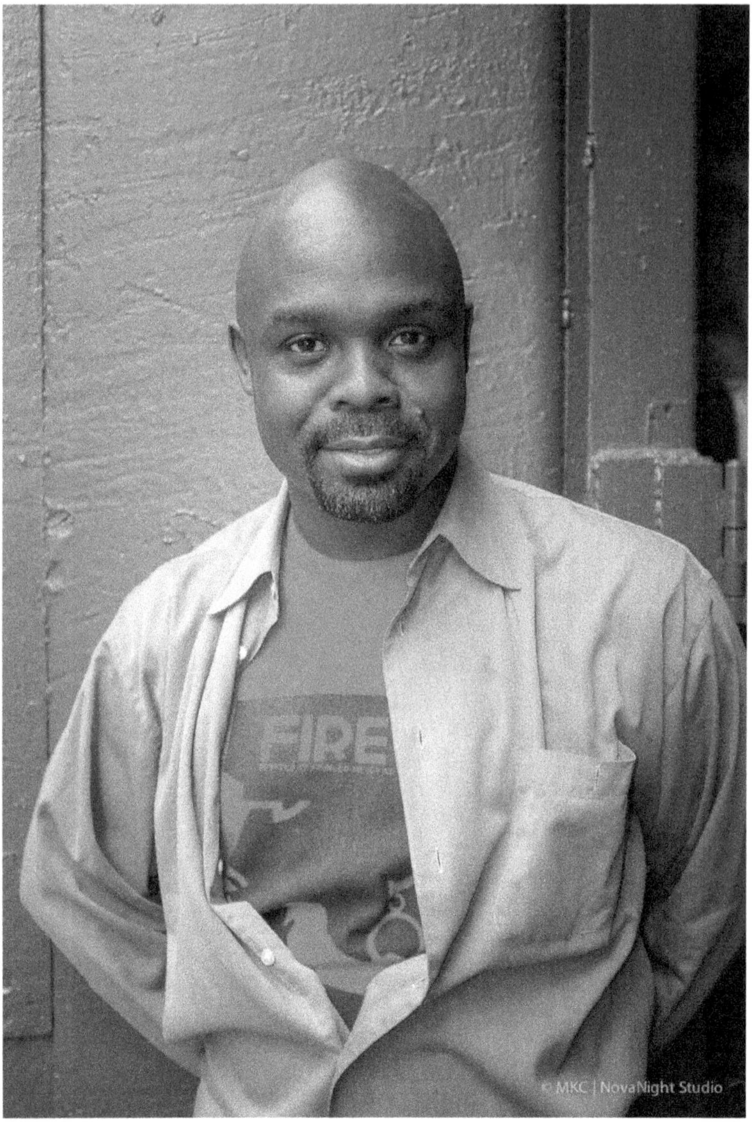

Robert Gibbons moved to New York City in the summer of 2007 in search of his muse-Langston Hughes. Robert has performed all over New York City.

His first collection of Poetry, Close to the Tree was published by Threes Rooms Press and can be purchased at :

www.threeroomspress.com

You may contact Robert
via his FaceBook presences :

www.facebook.com/anthonyrobertgibbons

www.facebook.com/jamesmercerlangstonhughes

longing for an unknown lover

when I think of you

I think of Nabokov

and Death in Venice

the way

I push my fingers

across the page

of your

private parts

inside creating

high art

making a climax

the way

I push this pen

Central Park

it was only yesterday
I sat on a bench
in Central Park West
the curvature of lips
of the lake
reminds me of
the higan cherry
the blaring
aviary; how we just
kissed by accident
maybe the mint julep
and the blossoms
the tussle of the leaves
in cotton white
that blow the fragrant show
of color and the water lily
those hints we share
as we au pair
there is no sunshine
it hides
beneath its blanket
only the banks
estuary is naked
there are gravel rocks
and boats to be docked
the days are shorter
sort of in a mood
for winter.

overture for a fugitive love

had me stranded in these February snows

rushing to the attic near Elwyn's quarry

the bauble heads of mosaic quilts and relics

we hide away in the winter; the smell

of the old; the bright rinse of snow spray

when it retreats; so I hide myself behind

the bay window; the fifteen steps to get

to me; only the traces of the empty

toothpaste and returned dishes; the

faucet left running reminds me; the

times and wind blinds me; so I wait

for another season in this maple red

night; where the twisting of shell white

and both of us are buried beneath ice

and it is cold here; it is cold here.

muse hotel

it takes a late night walk
off- off Broadway too times square
with enough of those
revolving doors and smelly carpets
casting couches and magic rabbits
just a walk near Madison
were the lights are up all night
the site of a tour bus and enough
with Porgy and Bess and
the Gershwins; the sin lives
in Hell's Kitchen near the Kit –Kat Club
and Mama Foo Foo is blowing bubbles
women in fuchsia cat suits
will get in trouble

the night has started around mid-
summer dreams and the beginning
lines of people in the bar upstairs
from the cabaret with clinking
glasses of Chardonnay
almost stepped on your breast
like some of those flyers from Chicago
a feisty type that's a rider
but did not have a lasso
don't use the terms cowboy
or down low.

Neetu
Wali

Hi! I am Neetu. Who am I? This question is very difficult to answer.

Well! If you insist, let me reveal. I am a human and like every other human I eat, sleep, drink, dance, sing, laugh, smile, cry and so on. Hang on! There is a difference. Unlike most of the human beings, I breathe and when I breathe, I relax. When I am relaxed, I draw. I draw sketches of me in words.

I have been orbiting around sun for forty years now. I started this journey on the Valentine day of 1974. I have seen people craving for heaven and I was born in the only heaven on earth (Kashmir). My Grandfather was a spiritual personality and a renowned poet of his time. Though he left me around 35 years ago, I couldn't let him go. I carry him in my eyes and mind and will do that till the end of my life. I hate words, yet I am full of words. I know words cannot express, yet I express me through words, because they are the only medium I am familiar with. That is why I try to express me as much as possible with as minimum words as possible.

When I did Masters in business administration, I never knew, writing will be the only business in my life. More than hobby writing is a necessity for me, because it helps me get the load of thoughts off my head. I don't remember when it that I wrote my first poem was. But I surely know the time of my last poem. Surely, not before my last breath.

Love

I asked a dove
What is love?
Birdie smiled and asked
Whose love?
Ok---- let it be my love
I replied with a surprise
Down bowed the little head
Face spitting gloom
Tears rolling down
I am here
Bound and inside
A small stinky cage
This is your love
He said in a breaking voice
Then what is love
I enquired, my eyes
Starting to open wide
You see me fly in the sky
Vast sky and fresh air
Shiny stars and glowing moons
This is how
My God loves me
Then why he lets me cage you
I asked, sadness in my eyes
He never lets you do it
You do it against-----
Before the bird could finish
Something inside me
Opened the door of my heart
And the bird flew away

Love and Perfection

What is evoked by perfection
Is not love
Simply impression
That's why the feeling
Is never deep
Always on the surface
That can be rubbed swiftly
By a gentle wave
Of the life sea
Love is the honey in bee
Sweetness in a fruit
Scent of a fruit
That is beyond perfection
And blind to perfect

Earth has no eyes to cry
yet absorbs the tears of sky
Beautiful flowers and sweet fruits
Precious gems and priceless stones
A befitting gift
For such level of
Level and perseverance

Sometimes I Think

Sometimes I think
what do I value more?
Your lust for me
Or my love for me
If my dreams are mine
Should they be about me?
Sometimes I think
What do I value more?
Your desires for me
Or my wishes for me
If my desires are mine
Why do I give up mine
For the sake of you
Your image of me
Or the real me
My prayers for me
Or my feelings for you
Whenever I pray
Why does my world
Gets reduced to you
Sometime I think
What do I value more
My faith in you
Or the man in you

Shareef

Abdur

Rasheed

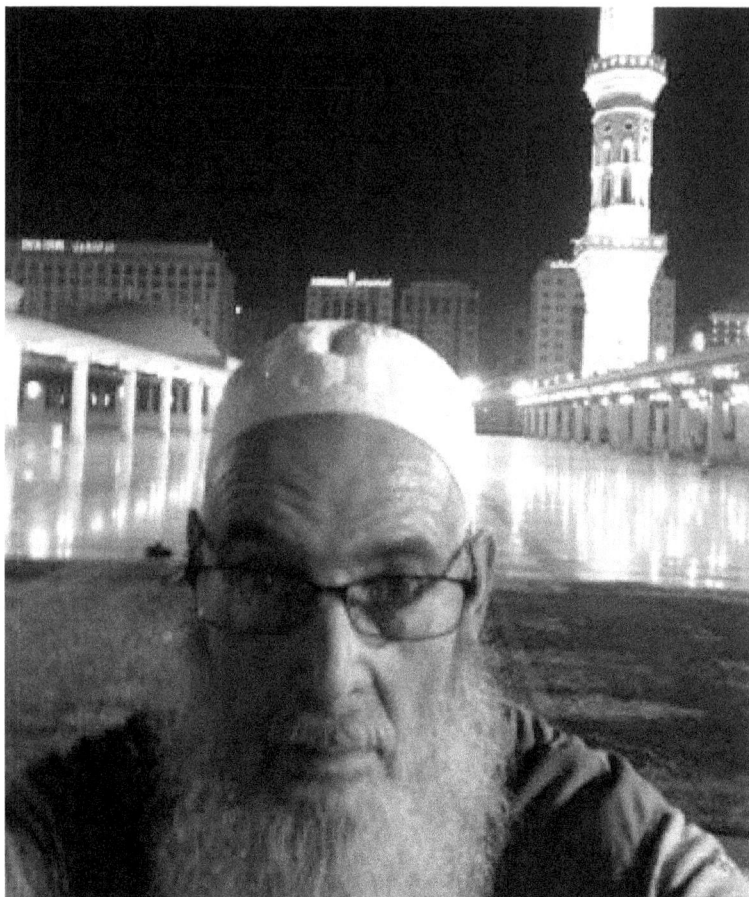

Shareef Abdur-Rasheed,AKA,Zakir Flo was born and raised in Brooklyn, New York. His education includes Brooklyn College, Suffolk County Community College and Makkah, Saudi Arabia. He is a Veteran of the Viet Nam era, where in 1969 he reverted to his now reverently embraced Islamic Faith. He is very active in the Islamic community and beyond with his teachings, activism and his humanity.

Shareef's spiritual expression comes through the persona of "Zakir Flo" . Zakir is Arabic for "To remind". Never silent, Shareef Abdur-Rasheed is always dropping science, love, consciousness and signs of the time in rhyme.

Shareef is the Patriarch of the Abdur-Rasheed Family with 9 Children (6 Sons and 3 Daughters) and 42 Grandchildren (24 Boys and 18 Girls).

For more information about Shareef,
contact or follow him at :

http://www.facebook.com/shareef.abdurrasheed1

http://zakirflo.wordpress.com/

http://www.innerchildpress.com/shareef-abdur-rasheed.php

https://www.facebook.com/pages/Muslim-Writers-Forum/370511683056503

Ships..,

that sail away,sometimes sink
getting away,on the way to
some illusional place
ride that glides at a dilusionall
pace
a particapant in a meaningless
race
sink deep in the drink
never again to be seen
just as they came,appeared
on the scene,never before
known of or seen,these ships
of various types
sometimes preceeded by
various degrees of hype,like..,
oooh how nice,get on board,
don't think twice or even think
at all
eventually they sink in the icy
drink
with all aboard these ships
not exclusively but including..,
relation*ships*,
a very curious vessel unique
a very different makeup to speak
of
unlike conventional craft should
be built on trust,,honesty,love!
consists of,transparency,sacrifice,
consideration and more
ideally would be nice if it's

all of the above before one boards
the relation**ship** to embark
on a perilous trip on this journey
called life
hark i hear another vessel appear
and then disappear into the vast
sea at night!
glide on the waves like a bird in
flight!
beware the relation*ship* that slips
away as sudden as it came,
appear then disappear as
though never here!
into the vast sea at night!
into this sea of life!

food 4 thought!

less..,

self and more us
in the key of trust
what a relationship
makes in the process
of give 'n' take
selflessness is what it
takes!
to prevent regress
dismiss fake!!
selflessness is what it
takes!
what a relationship makes!
takes mad respect, immense
always conflict avoid!
makes no sense!
when people lack..,
all of the above, devoid
love and happiness takes
a hit!
with..,
no selflessness, respect in
it!
selfishness makes a mess of it
Wiseman say..,
better to give then take
makes sense
relationships always hang in
the balance
never far from being at stake!

soo..,
to keep love afloat
use whatever floats your boat
but..,
remember for goodness
sake to invoke that
in relations selfish, folk clam up
like shellfish
dem dat respect choose!
get success, for instance
assistance from above
never lose love!
be.., blues free!

food 4 thought!

EggShells!!

Like steppin' on Eggshells
attitudes are more fragile yet
today's smile, tommorrow
flipped the other way around
never know what your gonna get
shrinks go to drink tryin to expound
on the mystery of how we think
like steppin' on eggshells
how do you step on eggshells?
it's a fact no matter how you
step on eggshells they will crack
you ask are relationships more fragile?
Yes! once you get past the ass and a smile
what remains to make it last awhile?
is substance there to past the test
to cement a bond beyond the flesh?
in reality it remains a fact, if you bet on
someone being there to take your back
because of mankind's unpredictable mentality
like eggshells no matter how you step
they will crack!
a cold hard fact!!

food 4 thought!

Kimberly Burnham

An Integrative Medicine practitioner, Kimberly Burnham uses poetry, words, coaching and hands-on therapies to help you heal. A published poet in several Inner Child Press anthologies, including Healing Through Words and I Want My Poetry To, Kimberly is winner of SageUSA's story contest with a poem about her 2013 Hazon CrossUSA bicycle ride. She is writing The Journey Home about that 3000 mile expedition.

Now, you get to be her muse with a list of seven experiences you yearn for. She writes a poem as if already, you are feeling the exhilaration of living your dreams.

You can find Kimberly ...

http://www.KimberlyBurnhamPhD.com
http://www.linkedin.com/in/KimberlyBurnham
http://www.amazon.com/Kimberly-Burnham/e/B0054RZ4A0

A Life Lost

So sad
I look
at death
not a movie
real and tragic
pondering ways
to change the world

People who feel better
make healthier choices
for themselves
their family
the community
our universe

What can I do
a horizon of wiser choices
helping him experience healing
bring a smile to her face

More experiences
on the way
as if my hand a salve
soothing connections
with one word,
gesture
action today

Do You Believe in Mother?

Together in a sac
shared genetic potential
growth watered with love
food and shelter
a similarity of nature
nourished by one woman's body

Do you believe
in change after delivery
if you listen quietly
you can hear mother
she exists all around us

Environment nurturing
the will sustains generations
the egg that becomes me
was in my grandmother

Miasms of what passes
generation to generation
the beyond surrounding
genetic make up

I chose one day
to inhabit
it is not all of me
what you see today
there is a part of my grandmother
and my great grandfather
and all who loved them

Carousel of Happiness

Would that life
is as easy as
buying a ticket
on the carousel of happiness

Fly into the past
meeting a lover
hurt by your actions
hiking in the mountains
above Boulder
with two big dogs

Talking out all the angst
making right all the hurt
expressing all the love
trapped
by two headed monsters
fear and insecurity

Walk into the beautifully arrayed
mountain store
pull out a dollar
pockets of success
smooth it out
exchange
a colorfully laminated ticket
for the carousel of happiness

Wait in line for your turn
to pick the wise panda
hand carved by a solder
returned from the Vietnam war
imbuing the wood
healing the scars of conflict

Listen to the soul soothing music
the Wurlitzer restored
ancient beauty
skilled loving hands
crafted paintings
drawing your eyes
into the scenes
as you ride
the carousel of happiness

Knowing your presence
your dollar
funds spinning
whirling joy
love in children's lives
peace and friendship
with the broken past

Loving every minute
you spend
on the carousel of happiness
tucked away at the pinnacle
of a lush green mountain.

William
S.
Peters, Sr.

Bill's writing career spans a period quickly approaching 50 years. Being first Published in 1972, Bill has since went on to Author 24 additional Volumes of Poetry, Short Stories, etc., expressing his thoughts on matters of the Heart, Spirit, Consciousness and Humanity. His primary focus is that of Love, Peace and Understanding!

Bill is the Founding Director of Inner Child Enterprises as well as the Past Director of Publicity for Society Hill Music.

Bill says . . .
I have always likened Life to that of a Garden. So, for me, Life is simply about the Seeds we Sow and Nourish. All things we "Think and Do", will "Be" Cause and eventually manifest itself to being an "Effect" within our own personal "Existences" and "Experiences" . . . whether it be Fruit, Flowers, Weeds or Barren Landscapes! Bill highly regards the Fruits of his Labor and wishes that everyone would thus go on to plant "Lovely" Seeds on "Good Ground" in their own Gardens of Life!

to connect with Bill, he is all things Inner Child :
www.iaminnerchild.com

Personal Web Site
www.iamjustbill.com

i am looking for you

i looked for you in the garden
and i knew you were there
for i could smell
your sweet fragrance
permeating the air
so i breathed deeply
that i may have more of you
within me

the flowers were blossoming
noting your presence
for your essence
has that effect
on life
so i sat and watched
the magnificence
of you
causing bloom
making room
for the heart of man
to engage
in your beauty

i heard the children's laughter
and i knew your joyful smile
was the cause
for all souls love
dancing with you
as i do
as i am now
in my thoughts of you

i felt your melodic touch
as you evoked a music
i can not describe
begin to play in my heart
filled with an incurable expectation
of embracing you again

the gentle breeze tickled me
into a new consciousness
as it whispered your name
into the ears of my eternal soul
and i smiled
for i remembered our when
as if it were our "Now"

i am tenderly licking my lips
being enraptured
by the moments when the twain met
yours and mine
with a caressing wantonness
and tender mercies

my eyes burst with color
and a quixotic kaleidoscopic wonder
and i too smiled and giggled
like the children
who only played with their innocence
for they knew not of device

i too blossomed
like the flowers
as i inhaled deeply
and held you within my breast
and i shall not breathe
a sweetness
quite like this again

i am looking for you
in the garden

ever for

my soul joyfully weeps in anticipation . . .
of your coming
…home.
i know with all due certainty
that you bear for me a bountiful heart,
filled with the gifts of "Heart",
with no limitations.

Through many restless nights
i rode the dream streams
of colorful light beams
looking over the horizons
of my aspirations . . .
lookin for you

All my senses enlivened
with the urge but to be of you . . .
through you . . .
in you . . .
once again . . .
for you complete
the "me" of "me".

Over the eons
i have watched
the waxing and waning
of my passions and desires,
knowing that only your heart
could align my path with my truth.

Need i say that
the warm velvet of your ethereal touch
grounds me in the soil
of the garden of "Birth and Death"
exposing my silly illusions . . .
that i am finite.

Yes Love,
in my delusional haste to live
and the creations of my own hauntings,
i knew you were always there . . .
heart in hand
flowing with the essence of all life
. . . love.
For with Love,
Death willingly is trumped
and thus submits it's veil of deceit
to what "IS" . . . Life!

So. my dear
bring me the breath of "BE"ing that sustains us . . .
bring me the Joy Divine
bring me my Life's Light . . .
Light my Lantern once again
bring me our life
that permeates all "BE"ing . . .
that i may awaken
and be transformed in the . . .

ever for.

on the "Fair Ways" of Life

i met you upon the fair ways of life
the day was bright and bonny
we made acquaintance
we shared smiles
and "get to know you" conversation

we parted that day
but only for a while
for we made plans
to redress the address
of me knowing you
you knowing me

you see, it seemed
that love was perhaps getting a chance
to be redeemed
in our encounter

we spoke on the phone
and we shared our loneliness
as we decided
we no longer wished to hide
out from life
so we made a date
and God, just like you
i could not wait
so i invited you over

you came at 7
i was prepared
i was expecting heaven
and that is what i saw
when i opened
my door for you

damn you were beautiful
in all my blinded ways

but
little did i know
that the seed you had to sow
in my garden
was such a bitter fruit

you brought darkness
to my door
and you and your
convoluted disparaging angst
crossed my threshold
i felt it
yet still
i invited you in
cause i thought i needed you

we sat,
we talked,
we smiled the polite smiles . . .
we even laughed
and we . . .

and though the warning signs
were prevalent
i was lonely
and i needed someone
to touch
to hold
to share with
and hopefully
enfold
into my heart

so we pressed on

moved on
from 7:00 that evening
to the new dawn
to breakfast

it was all happening
so wonderfully fast

time skipped forward
and i thought
we were going toward
accomplishing
the vision of lovers
you know
that happily ever after
filled with love
and laughter

that was all i could think of
being loved
the right way
day and night

you were my objective
my fixation
the elation
of my dream come true . .
or should i say
the "we" in you and i
was where i wanted to be

you see,
i have been waiting
praying
anticipating
that this day would come
to my life

you know what i'm saying
i ain't playing
this shit was and is serious

and you came along
with your sweetness
your song
and i forgot who i am
who i was
cause
i was seriously delirious
furiously curious

like a man on a desert
i had desires
fires inside
that needed attending
i was broken
and i needed mending

but like so many other times
i put my trust
in the wrong things
i put it in you
instead of me

had i knew
we would come to this
i wonder now
would i have
sought that first kiss
that lead us down this road
while hoping for bliss
to ever be

damn i miss
the possibilities

of what could have been

but for me
like so many more of us
like i said
we trust in the wrong things
we trust in our head
our thinking
while slowly sinking
only to hold in disdain
the thoughts
that led us astray

many times i was aware
and there was a certain fear
that embraced my clarity
and the doubt and disparity
that loomed as a possibility
i would not have it
so i denied it
defied it
and now . .
i cry over it
shit !

the temporal delusions
were a happy place
with a happy face
yet in the end
the taste of the fruit
i now eat
is not sweet
nor replete
save for the lessons delivered

and i remember
those seemingly right turns
that i now see as wrong turns
and the road burns
along the way

but i must confess this
that even though
the bliss was an illusion
as is this confusion
i now speak about
i have no doubt
that i am the better for the experience
and for that i thank you
for through you
i have found another
piece of me
and hopefully i can learn to see
more of me
and less of that
glitz shit
on the "Fair Ways" of Life

June

Features

~ * ~

Shantelle McLin

Jaqueline D. E. Kennedy

Abraham N. Benjamin

June Features

Shantelle
'elle'
McLin

Shantelle 'elle' McLin

"I like to believe that I have become the artistic magnet. In my lifetime, I've managed to meet incredible, sharp, intelligent, creative, imaginative, highly-motivated, inspiring, "gifted", shining people. My opened mind and adoring heart has become the center-piece to my existence. I believe in others so much, that I have dedicated my life to motivate, to flick the flame inside that individual... whereas that light inside sparks, and the true illumination of brilliance is seen."

Shantelle 'Elle' McLin is the co-creator and website administrator at www.ellemclin.com (A Shared Format 4 Poets), it is a blog website that features over 130 poets and over 1500 poems. Author McLin has two poetry books with Inner Child Press, *My First Poetry Book* and *Beyond Nursery Rhymes: Real Life Tales*.

Elle is a poetess by destiny's design, discovering that the purpose of her gift is to help heal, not only herself but others who may have traveled down the same darken path. You'll find that most of her written expressions are true to life because they are real life interpretations. Elle has been writing poetry since 1988 when she discovered vintage treasures in an outdated library.

You May reach Elle McLin . . .

Facebook
https://www.facebook.com/wwwellemclincom

Website
www.ellemclin.com

Twitter
@ElleBoogi

The Key...

It was a day that felt so thick, mortally impure
A day my mind had played its tricks and left me quite
unsure

Sound waves had hit the air, left with deafening rings
My ears just weren't the same, the muddling range of
things

In my heart I held a key, the one I wish to offer
That locks a book to all my secrets and yet I'm not the
author

Scripted deception which wish to hostage me
And yet still I grant access, by turning over the key

Those fabrications cannot harm me; for I am revised in
truth
And my past will not haunt me, the things I did in youth

Yesterday I saw a rainbow, within clouds cold and grey
Although the sun was absent, the warmth was present this
day

My smile was hidden within my thoughts, while chancing
on happiness
I thought I felt his love for me, possibly the confusion of
his kiss

I searched my heart for its key, and threw it faraway
That day I set myself free, to chance on love another day

The Truth about Love

Beyond the butterflies
In the pit of my stomach
Beyond the fresh blooming
Of love's roses
Is a love of supposes

In the crevice of delirium
When the newness fades
And we are playing a game of charades
Guessing how the other feels
Beyond the appeal
Beyond the doting feelings
There lies the truth about love

In truth, love is both hills and valleys
The path not always smooth
But the walk together creates the groove…
As emerging from the honeymoon phase
And graduation to testimonial praise
Of where we been and what have endured
Love seems both the illness and the cure

"He's No Good" Blues

The Blues sung on the radio,
It soundtracks remembered pain,
And it celebrates…
The releasing of it

I sit with wine in one hand
And ready to spike it with rum from the other
Getting in this "he's no good"… groove
Lord knows I tried what I could
But… "He's no good" gotta shake my head and toast to
that!

There seems to be desperation in these eyes,
They just want one good tear to fall…,
Waiting until I realize,
Why would I be crying over a no good man!
Had to cheers myself to that one

So I let Bobby Blue Bland belt out those notes.
Got into my "goodbye no good of a man" groove
Swaying side to side as I…
Listened away to me some blues…

Melodies of Pain

With wine glass in her hand,
a limp wrist,
and the long stem
resting between two fingers and her thumb,
she tilts the glass to her glossed lips.

As she taste the last drop,
eyes rolls in her head from appeasing delight.

One long sip to wash away the pain,
or at least to bandage it.

One sweet sip
of slightly aged mixture
of fermented grapes and peaches.

"Strumming my pain with his fingers", she sings.

"Killing me softly with his words,
killing me softly" she mellowed into a cry.

His words were both gentle with a touch of sting
from their reality.

Still fresh, his words oozing over her frame,
injection inside her mental, and creating tear storms.

She takes the glass
and tops it off with the mostly emptied bottle.

Humming now... "Ain't no man like the one I got..."
straight paused.... "Well, had!" and she downs this glass as
well.

The wine would only be her numbing agent for the moment,
to pacify her merely while stupor for the night.

His absence was only 13 hours,
4 minutes and 23, 24, 25 seconds and counting.

Seemed like a lifetime, as loneliness crept in,
then dived in to make an even more grand entrance.

"Perhaps he'll come to his sense", she said,
as she set her cup delicately to the table.

"Hell, perhaps I'll come to all my sense," she then mumbled,
as she picked up her glass and slammed it to the wall.

Weeble-wobble we all fall down, but hell, I think I'm gonna get up!
With mascara ruined and a tear-stained raccoon mask now appearing from her
off and on cries, she realized if he's the one, he'll coming running back.
Until then, she refused to take another sip, or allow another tear to fall over him.

The one before him, she boozed herself up when they were no more,
as she recognized her pattern,
she knew she did not want to re-fall into that trap
of a 'no good of a man' blues.

She changed the dial within her head... started singing jazz,
and scatted her way into the bathroom to cleanse her face.

"It's a new dawn, it's a new day, it's a new life... for me",
the last words she sung before she fell asleep!

Don't Wanna Be Sober

With all this love for my man, it becomes intoxicating
I come to be a bit tipsy
And a little dizzy in love
He got me tripping over my feet
Clumsy in his gigantic smile and his mesmerizing presence
Got me stumbling over here in his real love essence

I feel the butterflies in my belly
My knees weak, my legs like jelly
And when he comes close
Giving me a dose
Of his whew... lip lock--- I melt
Because his soul is felt
Intertwining and combining emotional concoctions of
intense passion
Telling him this kind of consumption needs to be rationed

While under the influence in his addictive flames
And tongued tied on his name...
I feel flutters
This waving sensation in my tummy
Got me flip-flopping and diving in the ocean of wino love
Riding out these ripples
Adoring the currents because that is the way love flows
And I tell you, each night my desire grows

I am so caught up inside his heavy gin & tonic, bionic
motions
His lovemaking is 180 proof
Immobile off his bourbon elixir tangling-of-the-sheets fun
Stupor from liquored passion rum
I am way past lit from his Absolut 'real-love' vodka
He is the intoxicant my body needs
And I am sorry, but no meetings are necessary

While boozed-up in his firm and concentrated hold,
I completely malfunction and he has all control
He is my melody and here I am humming his songs of
adoration
I am a lush for his tenderness, there is no moderation

My self-discipline when in his company is nonexistent
Because his soft touch can bring on tingles
Have me hammered and in a zone
Sending mental and physical vibrations
That can last all night long
Inside potent heated fluctuations... directed to my nerve
sensations
Transporting chills and again... intoxication

I am inebriated from his love
A drunken monkey that just can't get enough of... it
And I don't ever wanna be sober

Jacqueline
D. E.
Kennedy

Jacqueline Kennedy

Jacqueline D. E. Kennedy was born and raised in Louisville, Mississippi. Her family moved to Chicago, Illinois when she was 12 years of age. She has lived in California, Florida, Indiana and now resides in Tulsa Oklahoma. She was married at the tender age of 17 and is the mother of 4 children. She also has eight grandchildren.

Jacqueline aka Venus Sunshine enjoys writing poetry and has been doing so since the eighth grade . . . over 30 years. She is an avid journaler. She is a great supporter within the poetry community. Her voice is uniquely hers. If you would like to read more of her works, you can do so via her FaceBook Notes at :

https://www.facebook.com/suynshyn.kennedy

Reminiscing

As we're walking down Lake Charles Listening to
The Louisiana Jazz greats Trombone Shorty,
Louis Satchmo Armstrong and the legends...
Your scent is like , walking into a fresh summers
Bath in the back woods of the Louisiana Bayou...

The sweet smell of gumbo prepared in cousin
Josephine's kitchen where customers would come
To get a free samples of it, teasingly passes, by
My direction as we're holding hands... I smile
Reminiscing of you~lifting me off my feet up

Into your masculine muscular arms ...I gazed
At the sexiest way the white of your teeth
Brings the pride and joy of your smile
Can make a crowd at the Saints game thinking
They've won before the game ever began~

You're such a rare gentleman and a fine piece of art
Look at you~with your seersucker powder blue shirt
Open for the cool summers breeze off the Bayou's
And Lakes...sleeves and khaki's rolled up your arms
And Legs just enough to walk through the scenic
Prairie byways~

The look on your face you give me can melt my heart
Which renders my surrendering every moment of
Me to you, as we kiss...you held my chin as delicately
And tenderly leaving me with a sweet erotic heart
Pounding daydreaming of a moment to be imaged for

Our next sentimental journey...you open up the door
For me from your beautiful 1941 Studebaker Lark
Convertible...that automobile still speaks
Long time memories of us...You walk around the back
flirtatiously touching the curves of the vehicle never

Taking your big dreamy bedroom eyes off me
As I open the driver side door, your eyes fall down
Upon my bosom, from leaning too far over releasing
The door handle...I smile... as you drive away
You take my left hand, ever so gently caressing it

Glancing at the 5 carat diamond ring given by you
From your Mother for your future bride to be
You pull me close to you while we ride with
Anticipation of Love pondering inside my heart
Of our trip to the next destination...(to be con't.)

Jacqueline Kennedy

Loving You In The Fall

I love when the Fall leaves
Free fall flows from the trees
Twirls down on our heads, face
And sweaters
It brings out the warm Happiness
Inside our Joyful Hearts of Love
we run in the bustling piles of
Fallen leaves Vibrant bursting
Colors of "Mother Earth's" canvas
painting our picture in Awesome
Technicolor of what love like ours
Has to show
the Spiritual light Of the universe
Is a guiding light to the Greatness
In our lives that we have to give
Not only for Us, but for All
You lift me so high above the
Clouds is where I lay
I love your Big Bear Hugs
When You run up behind me
So safe and cozy
Wrapped inside your arms
Don't let me go, let's hold on
To this moment and close our eyes
Smell the fall aroma of Cantaloupes
Pumpkins, and Cranberries
As I face you and look into your
Face, I know, this is the place
I want to live throughout the rest
Of my Wonderfully Blessed Days
With ...."YOU"~

I Wrote "Nice" Today

I wrote Beautiful today ~I wrote about the sunrise
and made the moon hide, filled the air with butterflies
and Honeysuckle, while birds chirped and sang as they
flew away into the fresh smell of evergreen

I wrote Happy today, watching the neighbors get out for
church and the football teams were huddled up
ice cream trucks ringing their bells for children with tiny
giggles, snotty noses and bouncy pigtails

I wrote Romantic today, a cute young couple sitting on
the edge of a fountain of cupids with arrows firing water
while they make future plans of marriage ahead
and elderly guys making check mate on one another
for the second week straight

I wrote Passionate today, I painted a picture of a nude
couple
that had no curtains or blinds to hide from, he was giving
her
a Mandarin Coconut Massage, touching every smooth, soft,
curved mound, fingers and toes...were all tasty and liked
by him...hmmm, he makes me want some of his Mandarin
Coconut Massage Oils...
Yes, I painted him Passionately beautiful
today and loved every touch of It ~

Jacqueline Kennedy

You made me Love You

I admired everything about him
his charm was so much to adore.
He enlightened my heart
as if a halo of warm light traced my silhouette
He made a smile appear upon my face
that I'd never seen since two years back
He told me things that no one else would know
about him at that time
I fell head over heels
of the plans we made for the future
I heard of all his dreams
I melted into his life with our hands held close
He took care of my emotions
because he said to trust him
He caressed my ego
my heart no longer ached from the pain in my life
that i suffered from my past , because at last
our love was one
he held me so dear to his heart from a thousand
miles away ...

Addicted To You

I wake up this morning
Your eyes penetrating mine
I kiss your lips, embracing me
Is all the wanting of you I crave
Everyday with you is absolute
Ecstasy
I want you more today then
Yesterday, and twice as much
Hungering for you tomorrow
You open my world by twirling
My pearl of satisfying sensual
Touches of pulsating vibrations
You tantalize my senses
You devour every moment of my
Thoughts when I think of you
I can't, Turn away I'm addicted
To you, you keep the fire burning
Through me feeling me up
with Passion in my soul
Your caresses like no other
you love me wrapped around
Your every daydream
Of you making love to me with
those pillow soft screams
Satisfying you, is my life
With you never to have you
yearning because you whispered
Bella' you're my Eternity
So I'll continue to take you
Through phases of seductions
While you embrace me saying,
"I'm Addicted to You"

Jacqueline Kennedy

Abraham
N.
Benjamin

Abraham N. Benjamin

Abraham Benjamin aka Honest Abe is a Brooklyn, New York native. He is an Author/ Poet and also a budding musician. He has released two books of poetry under his "Unlocked Thoughts of a Prophet's Temple's" Series," Humble Beginnings: A Saga Revised" and "Cussing A Curse With Worse Verse." "Spoken Soldier" is his third installment in this series. He also has a CD, released July 2011, called "Brooklyn's Lost Son: Prelude to the Road to Redemption."

To his credit, he has had his work published in college art magazines, and feature collaborative Spoken Word albums. He has progressed as a Spoken Word artist, featuring in such venues as Time Square Arts Center, Bridgeport Innovation Center, The Brooklyn Book Festival and the Harlem Book Fair. He has also won back to back collegiate slams at the Bowery Poetry Club. His most recent endeavors includes a feature at The Black Poetry Café Poetryfest, and a televised feature on the documentary, "Poetry TV presents The Cypher's Den" (Executive Produced by Eric "Crow" Draven)

Abraham Benjamin can be contacted at bookinghonestabe@gmail.com

It's About Love

Understand, me wanting to show you
How much my aura is burning to make your soul come
The essence of our grandparents love.
Squirt the knowledge all down my erect mental shaft.
Leave the sticky reminisce of how a man
should rapture your being as a whole...

Goddess that "teach me"
how to love song by Musiq was written about us.
I can talk all the shit in world about sexual prowess,
Conquering your lioness energy,
Making discs in your spine quake from my back shots;
Leaving back shocks, with these strokes of genius
I'm delivering.

But if there's no more than an animalistic connection...
You just getting the hack sex of
Undeserving dick demons of past
Fucked the shit out of you;
So is wanting more than filling
the God given bowling ball holes of you so wrong...?

It's my belief,
There is a time, person, place
and thing for everything/one.
But too many either hold back,
Or don't work hard enough to come hard to achieve it...
Especially with love;

But all I can do is my best as far as you're concerned,
See, you are poetry that's God's work
Common man's pen imitate on paper...
To claim you his perfection to insure theirs w/words

Their copy isn't right, because
When they write just go left field.
Parallel line kicking porn poets
F'n you up, down, side 2 side
With average creativity

They should know better than to
Waste 3-5 min. or 15-30 min sets
Of both your time and patience with;
But this is not bout...

Making you poetically, potentially pulsate
From your panties for my pleasure....
For the record, I could do that.
Though this is not the point I'm tryna prove.
Our "spiritual Exercise" can also consist of

An enticing stare....to humming
1 of your favorite love songs
On your neck with my lips...on your spot, there....
So hear...me....
But don't just listen...feel me....
Cause professing love to you is 4 play lip service
That a brother like me has never been satisfied with.
Words are powerful,
But reinforcing them with actions makes sensual
and moist magic happen in the mind, body and soul.
And I intend to have you as a whole.
If you'll let me...add to your happiness
So we can live together in destined, blessed bliss...
And put a permanent smile on your face.

My Oxygen to Her Flesh

Lady in my life...
You of Mahogany mind, body and soul
sing rhythm minus the blues.

Took me one lyric too long but followed the clues
Of black love that flourishes through our burdened hearts...
That we're in parts from,
Pre and post St. Valentine 's Day massacres
Both seemingly hard to recoup the pieces and parts,
So now that the chards of us have communed in unison
We've birthed a beautiful collage.
Filled with will and hope for the future
without a mirage-laced canvas of feelings
That God and the universe mandated.

You give and take a brotha's breath away,
Possessing that Pam Grier, Foxy Brown,
take no BS strong mentality...
I'm in awe of you.
The times you've told me how much I make you feel,
How much I make you feel,
Like a natural woman on an Aretha Franklin tip.

From the way I rub and massage
your back, neck, shoulders, stomach,
ass and those cute little feet;
To how well I stroke, lick, moisten
the entrance to your soul between the sheets...

Through the fussing and fighting at times
Though temporary is a part of our growth;
But I know that if I'm ever hanging from the edge
You'll drop down that reconciliation rope.
And don't think your man won't respond in kind!

Love, without action to follow
Is just a four letter word,
Fuck, with just action and lust without emotion
Is just a four letter word;
Time, without giving it to you as compensation
for opening your heart and soul to and for me,
Never dropping the value of your self-worth in my eyes...
It's just four letters...

So to my ordained better half,
Let's live by our actions...
making sure every word solidifies our bond...

This Woman
Her Ancestor's Freedom Aura

As soon as I entered the room
My eyes tasted her smile.
Nose swallowed her scent,
And mind brewed a hot bowl of dreams
From her aura,
With our future grandchildren seasoned in.

5 seconds away,
From telling this figure of natural beauty,
"Thank you in advance"
For giving my solar system of sorrows
New light, entering this lonely orbit
With your illuminating shine

There was something about her
That made my 3rd eye
Cry these words into my mouth;
Birthing an out of wedlock
Lyrical oasis she can give her soul permission to soak in.

With Scorpio tendency tears of liquid frustration leaking,
From this taunted brother's 3rd eye, I wonder....
If somehow my words touched her mind right
Would the treasure in her chest be mine..?

If so, would she love me for my manhood,
The hood in the man
Or just the man;
With the main ulterior motive,
To keep her heart from breaking again;

Like the past mind menstrual felons
To keep away the forsaking pain weather
Clouding the beautiful black sunrise in her
God intended,

I'm sure storms will come.
This we know for sure,
But tell me,
Can you stand the rain..?
Had me Hendrix my attention on her
Stuck in the purple haze,
She consumed me,
Jimi couldn't voodoo child tune my ears
Off this woman's voice;

I did not come here looking for love.
No, I did not come here looking for love.
But it found me at first sight like Mary j.
For some reason L.L.'s "around the way girl"
played in my head.

Convo was common, yet still uncommon,
Giving my mind an erection
my penis can't hold a candle to;
The touch of this natural goddess's hand,
And the way she gave me that ancestor freedom grin,
Channeled my déjà vu chakra,

Like 1965 bus boycotts, and mourning
over Malcolm's assassination together;
Like buying back our children
from white oppressors in the 1800s;
Like being the only black couple
allowed at the table of the last supper;
Like Obatala & Oshun's souls rebirthing through us;

At the tip of my tongue like,
Hollow tips to hearts brain matter
Shed in my chest,
Hitting infatuation top charts of our bodies at #2...
#1 is too overrated a number to claim this growing bond.
But a beast name, "caution" kept my soul train
From penetrating this,
Harriet Tubman's Underground Railroad;
Halting a journey we seemed destined for;

For real, like something was telling me beautiful disasters
Like solar eclipses,
To a man like me,
Should only occur once in a lifetime;

Though some risks are worth the profit,
And are pro-fits for prophets;
So this time the clouds will cry rainstorms of hope for us.
This woman, with a Coretta Scott entity of miracles.
This woman, with Isis
crevasse anointed masterpiece of phoenix.
Burning a sunder of emotions through my veins,
Ringing Bob Marley redemption tones
 in my mind, body and soul
Giving my heart permission to whisper to me,
"A change gone come"
Giving me the right to love, again…

Not Just an Apology
2nd Burn Notice

This poem is NOT just an apology....
It's a new offering....no promise,
Cause they made to break like No. 2's
But a guarantee....the burn notice of redemption
With the scarlet letters of A-B,
For the solace of D-E-B-B-I-E...

Your Trifecta scorched...Cries of a water Siren
Have repeatedly been spoken...
but deaf reverberation birthed my silent affection.
A proud Pisces to the bone...
though I seem to be the one lately acting fishy.
My lack of attention to your details showed you
The failure of a-male like e-mail accidentally sent to spam
Made you less of my female
with Oshun reincarnated love...
Only an Obatala in walking flesh can handle...
I can see why it's become easier to feel like
I've abandoned your heart...

When you took that pen...
...and ink laced earthly emotions
To sow this poet in,
To your soul's skin from many other men;
It sure wasn't a sin!!

Because you got me...via an engaging Pisces lure.
Not to the fact I maybe such a prize
But because you felt it was worth it in your eyes.
From when "Tongues were made" to
"How love was made"
While spending the night in Philly;
We loved/I loved....and still love you...
Before and after, I stay wanting more...
To get closer 2U...
And baby....I'm not ready for a detour.
Or return trip from the precious heavy
Possessed inside that chest of nostalgia unlocked;

Know,
That the significance of the intellectual,
giving nature of your presence....
Is a present and far from omnipotent...
And God knows love w/o or w/o enough action...
to back it up doesn't hold wait.
This piece of peace is not considered the bail $$
of verbal benevolence
For criminal acts of treason in our relationship;
Now a Grenadian boy with Caribbean dialect
On the verge of walking the plank,

"It's the simple things in life we forget...
She keeps on talking but don't hear what she said.
Why do we make something so easy so complicated...?
When it's all right in front of my face...
But I can't see it..."

Simplicity,
Of remembrance....is all that was asked.
To show devotion and dedication
And shouldn't need to pop a couple of Ginkgo pills...
Maybe if I did....wouldn't be
digging out this grave with word shovels.

Not sure if any what I'm saying
will redefine your ink to my pen...
Just on my Benjamin Franklin.
Flying a kite of geometric dimensions
Into your sky to electrify and solve
This equation of love together...
Braving the current stormy weather...
This is the kind of rain New Edition
asked if you can stand.

But like I said in the beginning...
This poem/prayer/letter is not an apology...
Failing the relationship etiquette
101 in these lessons of love…
It's an offering...no promise, but new guarantee
Toward a happiness that I BELIEVE
Is still destined for the times ahead…

Poet Malion Comfort

She is the pain release
My heart has tried to win
I've chiseled in her 4 ways
Putting in work like a blacksmith with my hammer pen
Carving with every puncture of my point
Into those padded walls;
So I continued grinding.
Till my fine point tip
Launched this anticipated ink of joy
Plastering those growing eyes I gave her
Noticing the satisfaction just painted on and
Around this masterpiece in the making.
Far from finished,
But half-way done
The sun of dreams
Splashed reality wishes
Her upper torso alive
Soaked in Mahogany pigment
Blazed with Nappy Nubian bristles
Pupils coated from God given midnight;
Looking like summer tasted this mold of clay,
Gargled to spit a Goddess image b4 me.
My legs like cinder blocks
Limbs covered with torment and shock.
This woman,
This entity of miracles,
This crevasse anointed master piece of Phoenix
Began chiseling me
Limbs back to LIFE!!

WHAT U-BER ILL VOODOO IS TAKING PLACE
IN THE PRESENCE OF MY PERSON?!
These fantasies birthed in my mind
Have bungee jumped
The walls of life imitating art
Art imitating life
With every stroke of my hammer
I hear Lucifer's whispers.
He couldn't create something so sinfully fantastic
Possessing Godiva features
Wearing ancestor freedom grins
Not even on his worse day.
How many of us can say
You've successfully broken
Silent chambers of loneliness...
With the Heavens and universe smiling
For you to believe in the impossible?
I'm a writer.
A Bandit Brother from Brooklyn.
That wants a love,
Needs a love
Like this...
All I have is
This metaphysical Masterpiece
Giving me Comfort.

Other

Anthological

works by

Inner Child Press, ltd.

www.innerchildpress.com

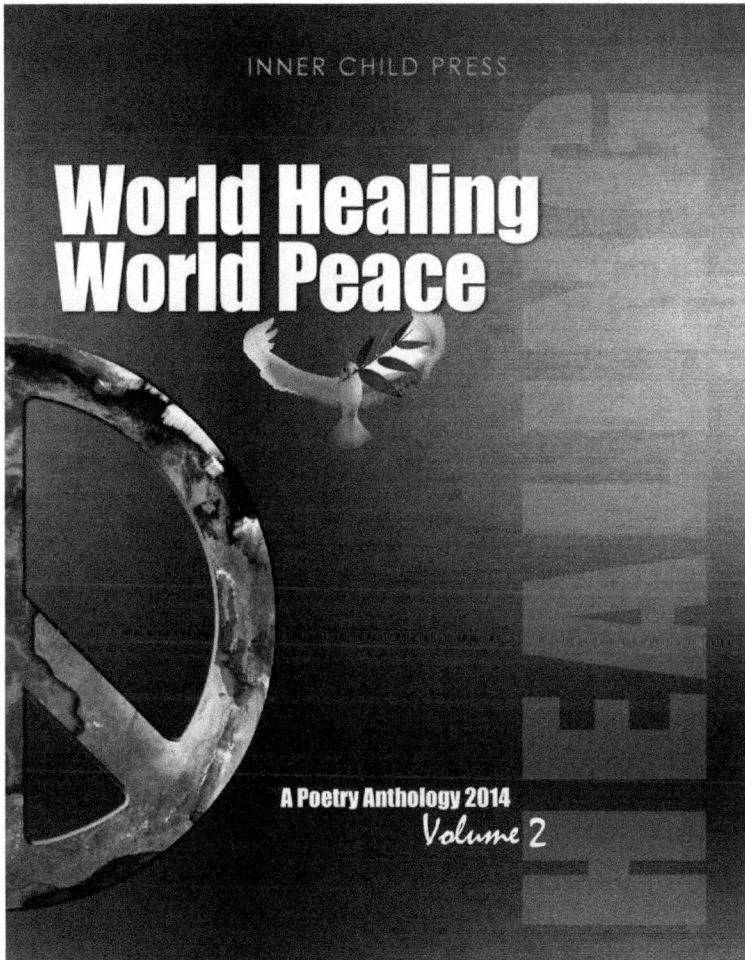

Inner Child Press
Anthologies

the year of the poet

May 2014

May's Featured Poets

ReeCee
Joski the Poet
Shannon Stanton

Dedicated To our Children

The Poetry Posse

Jamie Bond
Gail Weston Shazor
Albert 'Infinite' Carrasco
Siddartha Beth Pierce
Janet P. Caldwell
June 'Bugg' Barefield
Debbie M. Allen
Tony Henninger
Joe DeVerbal Minddancer
Robert Gibbons
Neetu Wali
Shareef Abdur-Rasheed
Kimberly Burnham
William S. Peters, Sr.

Lily of the Valley

Inner Child Press Anthologies

the Year of the Poet

April 2014

The Poetry Posse

Jamie Bond
Gail Weston Shazor
Albert 'Infinite' Carrasco
Siddartha Beth Pierce
Janet P. Caldwell
June 'Bugg' Barefield
Debbie M. Allen
Tony Henninger
Joe DaVerbal Minddancer
Robert Gibbons
Neetu Wali
Shareef Abdur-Rasheed
Kimberly Burnham
William S. Peters. Sr.

Our April Featured Poets

Fahredin Shehu
Martina Reisz Newberry
Justin Blackburn
Monte Smith

Sweet Pea

celebrating international poetry month

the Year of the Poet

The Poetry Posse

Jamie Bond
Gail Weston Shazor
Albert 'Infinite' Carrasco
Siddartha Beth Pierce
Janet P. Caldwell
June 'Bugg' Barefield
Debbie M. Allen
Tony Henninger
Joe DaVerbal Minddancer
Robert Gibbons
Neetu Wali
Shareef Abdur-Rasheed
Kimberly Burnham
William S. Peters, Sr.

March 2014

daffodil

Our March Featured Poets

Alicia C. Cooper & hülya yılmaz

Inner Child Press
Anthologies

the Year of the Poet

February 2014

violets

The Poetry Posse

Jamie Bond
Gail Weston Shazor
Albert 'Infinite' Carrasco
Siddartha Beth Pierce
Janet P. Caldwell
June 'Bugg' Barefield
Debbie M. Allen
Tony Henninger
Joe DaVerbal Minddancer
Robert Gibbons
Neetu Wali
Shareef Abdur-Rasheed
William S. Peters, Sr.

Our February Features

Teresa E. Gallion & Robert Gibson

The Year of the Poet
January 2014

Carnation

The Poetry Posse

Jamie Bond
Gail Weston Shazor
Albert 'Infinite' Carrasco
Siddartha Beth Pierce
Janet P. Caldwell
June 'Bugg' Barefield
Debbie M. Allen
Tony Henninger
Joe DaVerbal Minddancer
Robert Gibbons
Neetu Wali
Shareef Abdur-Rasheed
William S. Peters, Sr.

Our January Feature
Terri L. Johnson

Mandela

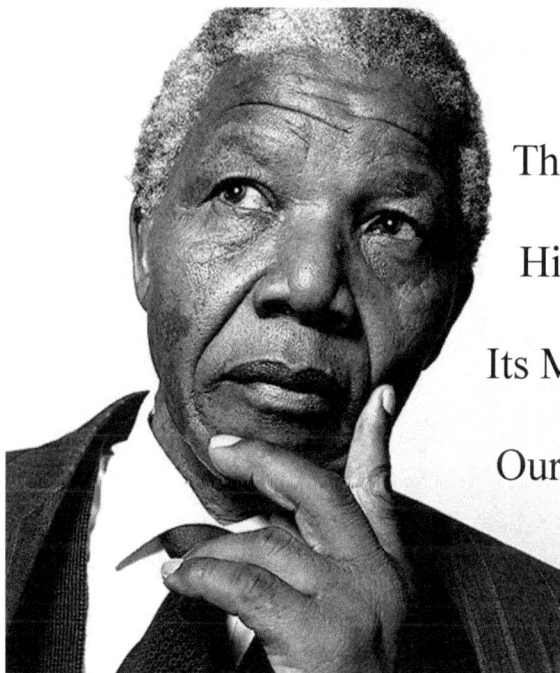

The Man

His Life

Its Meaning

Our Words

Poetry . . . Commentary & Stories
The Anthological Writers

Inner Child Press
Anthologies

A GATHERING OF WORDS

POETRY & COMMENTARY

FOR

TRAYVON MARTIN

2012

World Healing
World Peace

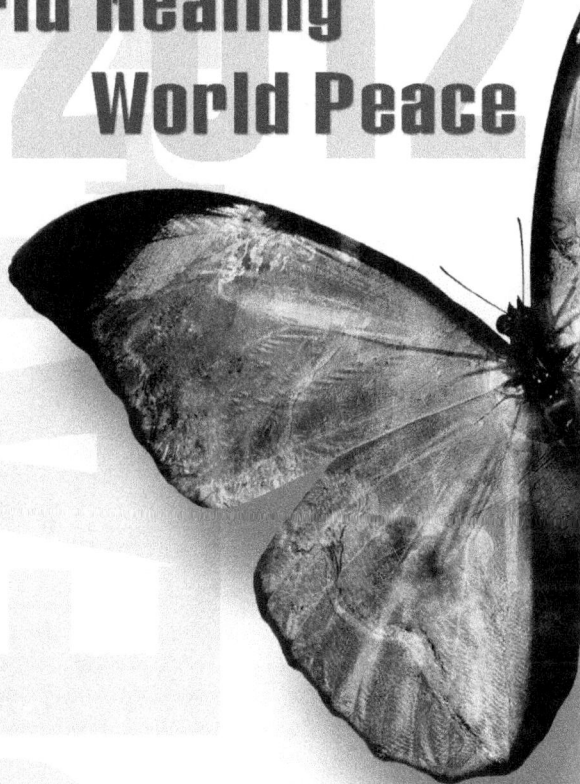

A POETRY ANTHOLOGY
Volume 1

Inner Child Press
Anthologies

World Healing
World Peace

2012

A POETRY ANTHOLOGY
Volume 2

healing through words

Poetry ... Prose ... Prayer ... Stories

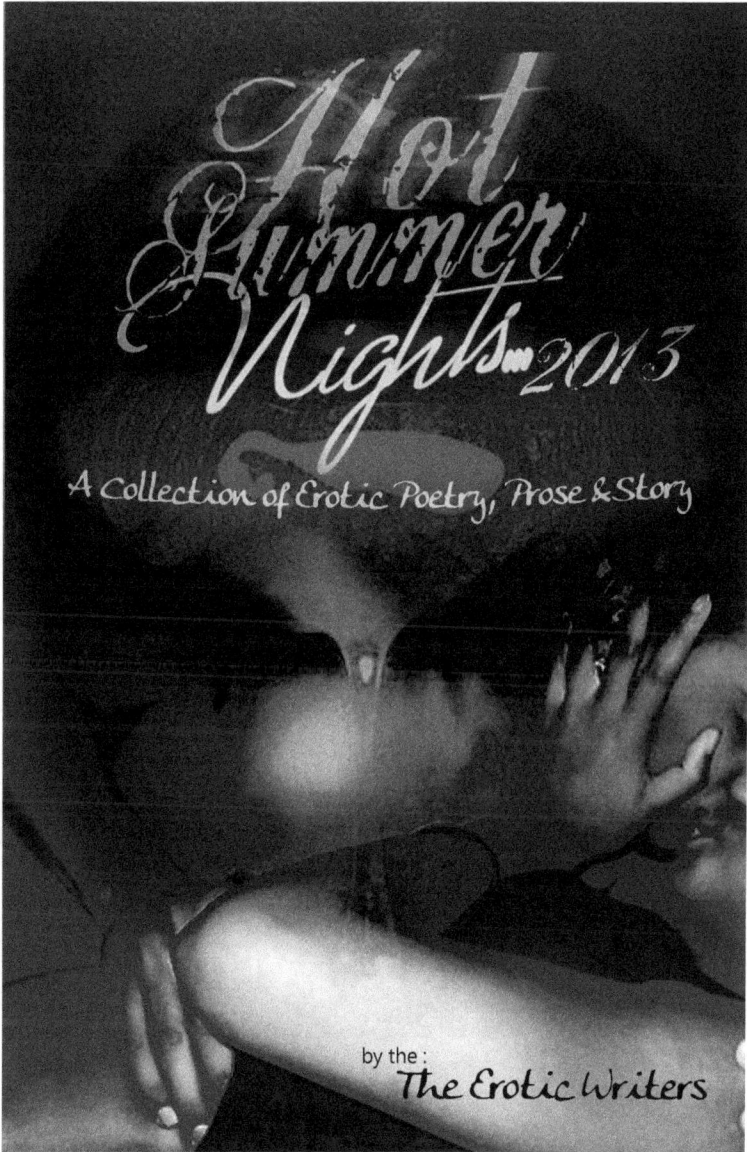

Hot Summer Nights... 2013

A Collection of Erotic Poetry, Prose & Story

by the :
The Erotic Writers

the

Valentine's Day

Anthology

poetry . . . prose & stories of Love

The Love Writers

Inner Child Press
Anthologies

i

want my

PoEtRy

to . . .

a collection of the Voices of Many inspired by …

Monte Smith

Inner Child Press Anthologies

a collection of the Voices of Many inspired by ...

Monte Smith

i want my

PoEtRy

to . . .

volume II

Inner Child Press Anthologies

11 Words

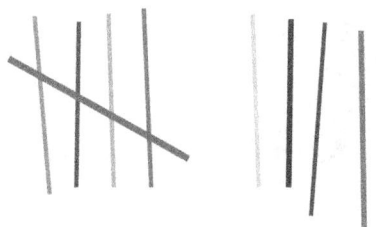

(9 lines . . .)

for those who are challenged

an anthology of Poetry inspired by . . .

Poetry Dancer

Inner Child Press
Anthologies

a

Poetically
Spoken
Anthology
volume I
Collector's Edition

Inner Child Press
Anthologies

and there is much, much more !

visit . . .

http://www.innerchildpress.com
/anthologies-sales-special.php

Also check out our Authors and
all the wonderful Books
Available at :

http://www.innerchildpress.com
/the-book-store.php

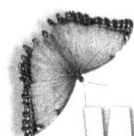

www.worldhealingworldpeacepoetry.com

Inner Child Press
Anthologies

TEE SHIRTS & HATS

4

SALE

Anthologies for Sale

WORLD HEALING ~ WORLD PEACE

$ 20.00

SMALL * MED. * LARGE * XL * XXL

www.worldhealingworldpeacepoetry.com

Tee Shirts for Sale

$ 22.00

http://www.innerchildpress.com/the-year-of-the-poet.php

Anthologies for Sale

COMBOS

$ 25.00

SMALL * MED. * LARGE * XL * XXL

FOR INTERNATIONAL POETRY MONTH ONLY

www.worldhealingworldpeacepoetry.com

Tee Shirts for Sale

COMBOS

$ 40.00

SMALL * MED. * LARGE * XL * XXL

http://www.innerchildpress.com/the-year-of-the-poet.php

Anthologies for Sale

COMBOS

$ 50.00

SMALL * MED. * LARGE * XL * XXL

http://www.innerchildpress.com/the-year-of-the-poet.php

Tee Shirts for Sale

THE YEAR OF THE POET

$ 20.00

SMALL * MED. * LARGE * XL * XXL

http://www.innerchildpress.com/the-year-of-the-poet.php

This Anthological Publication
is underwritten solely by

Inner Child Press

Inner Child Press is a Publishing Company
Founded and Operated by Writers. Our personal
publishing experiences provides us an intimate
understanding of the sometimes daunting
challenges Writers, New and Seasoned may face in
the Business of Publishing and Marketing their
Creative "Written Work".

For more Information

Inner Child Press

www.innerchildpress.com

Inner Child PRESS

Let Us Share
Our Magic With You

www.innerchildpress.com

FINI